EDUCATION

IN

A CHANGING WORLD

Essays on Teaching and Learning for a Better Life

Irie Glajar

EDUCATION

IN

A CHANGING WORLD

All Rights Reserved
Published By
Positive Imaging, LLC
9016 Palace Parkway
Austin, TX 78748
http://positive-imaging.com
bill@positive-imaging.com

ir_gl@yahoo.com

ISBN 978-1-944071-03-5

And so, my fellow Americans: ask not what your country can do for you — ask what you can do for your country. My fellow citizens of the world: ask not what America will do for you, but what together we can do for the freedom of man.

John F. Kennedy, Inaugural address,

January 20, 1961

Mr. Gorbachev, open this gate. Mr. Gorbachev, tear down this wall.

Ronald Reagan at Brandenburg Gate in West Berlin, Germany.

June 12, 1987

Never regard your study as a duty, but as the enviable opportunity to learn to know the liberating influence of beauty in the realm of the spirit for your own personal joy and to the profit of the community to which your later work belongs.

Albert Einstein

Also by Irie Glajar

"WE ARE ALL ONE, The End of All Worries: Scientific and Spiritual Testimonies to the Unity of All Things"

http://the-end-of-all-worries.com

"TEACH FOR LIFE, Essays on Modern Education for Teachers, Students, and Parents"

http://teachforlife.positive-imaging.com

"ESCAPE TO FREEDOM, Chronicles of a Life on Two Continents, My Escape from Communist Romania, An Autobiography"

http://escapetofreedom.positive-imaging.com

"2015 INSPIRATIONAL MATHEMATICS CALENDAR AND DAY PLANNER"

http://mathcalendar.positive-imaging.com

For details contact Irie at: ir_gl@yahoo.com.

Contents

Dedication and Thanks

This book is humbly dedicated to you, the readers. Thank you for your noble intent to improve your lives and the lives of others, and I wish you the best on this journey.

I dedicate these essays to my wife Valentina and my son Sergio. Thank you for creating the environment that motivated me to write this book; I am forever grateful.

And I dedicate EDUCATION IN A CHANGING WORLD to my great friends Jo and Flem. Thank you for all your help and appreciation. Your numerous positive editing suggestions substantially improved the presentation of many sensitive educational topics in these essays. Also, thank you for the back-cover inspiring praise that presents the book in its true colors.

Introduction

Modern life offers an impressive variety of fronts for improvement in what concerns human condition. Everywhere we look present situations can be improved. Nothing is perfect. At the same time we should not be content with a mediocre state of affairs. Therefore, a question is imminent: what is there to do to rise above mediocrity? As soon as I finished my *Teach For Life* book, I felt there was much more to include in proposed solutions to modern problems we face. This volume is just that: a collection of ideas meant as food for thought for a better life assuming we strive for excellence. Although the 34 essays included herein are very diverse, they can be clustered in a few main themes.

One of my favorites is the idea of 'meaning.' Is there meaning behind what we are and do, or is it all at the mercy of chance? As expected, the answer to this question makes all the difference in the world in terms of how we view and conduct our lives. Assuming there is meaning, intrinsically validates concepts of personal development, personal responsibility, and efforts to avoid negativity at all costs. Suddenly, self-growth becomes paramount in completing the picture of why we are here and where we are heading. In this respect, going within, reflecting on oneself and meditating can be great avenues toward accomplishing such worthy and noble goals.

A second selection of essays included here surrounds academic education. Since I worked as a mathematics instructor for 33 years at both secondary and college/university levels in the U.S., my experience drove me to express some of the stringent concerns I have about education in this changing world. From academic issues in the classroom and learning foreign languages, to learning by traveling, as well as the funding of education, there are many important themes that I feel need to be addressed in order to preserve and encourage dependable as well as improving education. Our intended mission should be to help generation after generation of students reach their highest goals.

The subject of mathematics captures a very special place in my heart, so I enthusiastically dedicate several essays to this wonderful field of modern education. As far as the teaching of mathematics is concerned, I believe that live classroom teaching by an experienced instructor is by far the best approach. I suggest that online and software mediated instruction should be kept as supplemental but not used as replacements for the long-term proven pedagogical lecture approach. This approach facilitates teaching the beauty of mathematics and its intriguing reflections in our universe in less intimidating and in user-friendly ways. Lecture can be a suitable avenue to help students enjoy and appreciate realities emanating from educational exchanges with international professionals, such as the two interviews included in here. Moreover, in classroom lecture settings, instructors can easily underline the importance of fundamental skills, as well as the wide range of ideas and interconnections in mathematics. At the same time, the lecture approach may make it easier for students to eradicate the proverbial fear of mathematics, and even replace it with love and acceptance for this essential field of modern education.

Teaching and learning are two main facets of the crucially meaningful evolutionary process in which humans aspire to happiness. We learn something new every day, whether we know it or not. However, our general aim is to acquire the information that will bring us comfort and happiness. That is why a significant part of this book includes ideas and suggestions on what we can do to reach the kind of living that brings us joy. After all, isn't the word joy a brief but great way to define the meaning of life? So, with all this in mind, we can set ourselves on a path of learning with the highest purpose: to reach that level of accomplishment and understanding that will allow us to be happy now and in every moment that follows, regardless of the circumstances of our lives. In the meantime, we should treasure every one of our steps along this path. After all, there should not be any desirable alternative to joy!

Consequently, I hope that the essays included in here can help the human longing for improvement in a variety of ways. In this respect, I believe that even those who feel content with their present circumstances can find within the covers of this book ideas that might motivate them to pursue changes for the better in their evolution through life. In the meantime, I do subscribe to the philosophical precept of "nothing is perfect," so I invite everyone to join in and embark on the train of self-improvement, such that in turn we can assist those around us who are also willing to help themselves.

1

Why Life?

By learning to contact, listen to, and act on our intuition, we can directly connect to the higher power of the universe and allow it to become our guiding force.

Shakti Gawain

The power of intention is well known as the engine at the core of human actions. In the beginning, any human accomplishment is an intention, a thought, a plan that details the accomplishment of the desired outcome. In this respect, perhaps the entire cosmos is the outcome of a great thought of a universal mind. Everywhere we look, we see living forms, from simple to complex, struggling to stay alive regardless of the circumstances in which they find themselves. Aside from the built-in law of entropy, only when conditions develop to unbearable levels, living forms die. Therefore, it seems reasonable to assume that, within this hunger for living, behind any intention manifested in the physical universe there should be a certain level of awareness, purpose, and/or intelligence, which drives its potential realization. In other words, intentions cannot appear accidentally.

In search for the origin of life on Earth, revelations in the realm of biology describe the innate tendency, or intent, of even sub-molecular entities, atoms organizing themselves in chemical bonds, to evolve and survive. The intention appears to be one of union, bonding to form more complex biological living structures, molecules, and then cells that divide themselves. Cell division is of particular interest since at this point cells want or intend that their 'descendants' inherit exactly the same characteristics as themselves! How would this be possible? The answer is clear: by designated dependable acidic molecules, the DNA. Now the crucial question seems to be inevitable: why? Why do cells, in a human embryo for example, want to divide and keep their genetic identity? The reason appears both logical and deeply profound: in order to form different tissues and organs, yet, to become an individually identifiable organism. The operating word here is *different*. What determines which cells will form what specific tissues and organs? Does this selection happen at random or do the cells already *know* their future? The science of today has no answer. Nevertheless, over eons, organisms thereby formed, eventually evolved into complex thinking and reasoning physical entities, and here we are human beings capable of asking the main question: WHY? Why life, and more importantly, why life at this level of sophistication?

Moreover, the new physics, the quantum physics, presents us with an equally stunning picture as we investigate deeper the composition of matter. The subatomic level of material existence, the level where particles organize themselves independently of any human direction (like the cell division previously mentioned), appears to be governed by laws of an invisible origin but nevertheless on purpose. In this respect, the famous "double slit" experiment indicates that the photon (the particle/wave smallest component of light) knows when it must pass through one slit (as a particle) or two slits (as a wave) to reach the screen, and acts accordingly, as it creates different projections. Within the same realm, one theory suggests that subatomic particles display some level of intelligence (awareness) in their manifestation: it appears that, in a pairing entanglement, they somehow instantly communicate the changes inflicted on them to their counterparts at a distance, regardless of the distance. In other words, we cannot study the changes on one of them without instantly observing the same changes in the other one far away, even thousands of miles away. The high amount of energy intrinsically inherited in subatomic particles (see nuclear energy) might justify such incredible ability and it might explain the obvious drive for life, for existence, for survival, and for evolution into more complex forms.

The question is again WHY? Why do all material forms known to us at this time in history want or prefer to keep living, to evolve into more complex and complicated entities? Isn't easier and 'more economical' to exist as the simplest possible components of the universe ... forever? As far as we can tell there is no effort, there is no struggle, and there is no 'pain' at that level. However, matter refuses to stay at the most fundamental stage of existence. Logically, then, it follows that there is a built-in intent to change, to combine, and to evolve into more sophisticated forms. Why? One could say that it happens 'accidentally' but the evidence may contradict such possibility. In this respect, I would like to suggest that 'accidental' and 'causal' are two mutually exclusive terms. Indeed, the laws of physics manifested in the known universe support a cause and effect nature, at least of the material world to which we belong. Although it can be argued that some conscious design may have included elements of random chance, I would like to suggest that any 'accident' or random event can be logically explained as the effect of a series of sequential causes (see *We Are All One*, my 2007 book). Consequently, it seems logical to claim a certain level of primordial intent that would ensure the evolution we witness all around in a cause and effect manner. But, an intent implies awareness, which takes us to the next hypothesis: it seems that there could exist an omnipresent intelligence at literally infinite strati of progressive levels of complexity, and it should be non-material. I say non-material because even before the smallest material entity was formed, it appears that there may have already been some purposeful guidance at work. Indeed, if modern physics theory is right as far as the origin of our universe is concerned, questions arise: what caused the Big Bang and why? We can see, then, that this guidance keeps being the driving force throughout the evolution of matter from simple to complex forms, culminating with, as far as we know today, humans who continue to evolve in an effort to better understand themselves and their universe.

Carl Sagan, the late well-known American physicist and astronomer, once said that we are a way for the universe to know itself. This might in fact be true. Humans might just be a link in an impressively complex universal scheme to intentionally build more evolved beings capable of asking the fundamental questions: who am I, why am I here, what is my place in the universe, and where am I going? The inevitable answers to these questions should be clustered around the effort to find a meaning for life, or at least for human life. In this respect, it seems that we are here to make sense of the universe through our existence. Perhaps the universe, immersed in the primordial intelligence that permeates all things - implicitly its own most fundamental parts - decided to know itself via material intelligent beings such as us, and to manifest this knowing in physicality versus only conceptually (immaterially). Consequently, seeing each other as implicit components of a greater whole with a purpose–the universe–life appears to make perfect sense. We can then understand our place in the larger scheme of things and we will think twice before rushing to immature judgment relative to other forms of life, and of course, relative to other human beings.

And Carl Sagan was not alone. Many other physicists from the last two centuries arrived to similar conclusions, as I presented in details in my 2007 *We Are All One*. Especially physicists of the 20th century who have set the foundation of quantum mechanics suggest that the universe appears to be more of a thought than a machine running out of steam as it has been presented within the frame of classical physics. In addition, supporting the same idea, there is a vast volume of inspired writings from the spiritual realm, which, via fundamental ideas from Eastern philosophy, finally connects physics with metaphysics.

Along these lines, the trilogy *Conversations with God* by Neale Donald Walsch presents a clear picture of inclusion and unity within a universal thought that I like to term the universal intelligence. The key idea repeatedly underlined in these *conversations* is that we cannot know anything without knowing its opposite –

reason why the opposite was created in the first place. It is, therefore strongly suggested that duality is imperially necessary in order to experience (know) anything. In other words, we cannot know that which is if we don't acknowledge that which it is not; or, in the absence of that which it is not, that which is, is not. So, we cannot know light in the absence of darkness, inside in the absence of outside, good in the absence of bad, love in the absence of hate, and ... being in the absence of not being (life in the absence of death). Indeed, this seems to be a paramount message received from both the new physics and the *conversations*: we may be a way for the universe to know itself (we are vivid elements of the universal intelligence), but to make that possible we first must know ourselves as not intrinsic parts of the universe. And in fact the separation paradigm that has been overwhelmingly dominating most of recorded history provides exactly this need for duality. However, over millennia, the human race slowly educated itself toward the realization that we are all one, and that is meant to finally show our real place in the universe.

In this respect, I think that the ultimate purpose of academic education is to help human beings understand their place in the world and society, and to make their lives positive and constructive experiences. In the end, students at all levels of education should turn out to be harmonious human beings in a harmoniously driven society. With the previously suggested understanding of the meaning of life, this prerogative should not appear as a too far-fetched goal, but should be held as a realistic possibility. Therefore, we should all view education as a necessary exposure to a conglomerate of ideas in a variety of subjects, meant to set a solid foundation for people to intentionally become the thinkers capable of saying: "I know who I am, I know why I'm here, and I know where I'm going." This realization will un-doubtingly lead to a level of human existence where citizens of the world will not strike at others domestically or otherwise. In return, this will open up a future of real progress toward the commendable level of peace, love, and understanding for which we all strive.

So, life in the universal scheme of things seems to impersonate that step intentionally taken by the omnipresent non-material intelligence in order to understand itself in the most basic and profound way: physically. Consequently, we human beings should be most proud of our role of thinkers and conscious participators in what *conversations* describe as the "only game in town," namely the interplay between the world of ideas, potentiality, and physical expression so vividly experienced via the five perceptional human senses. Let this realization help us all bring our meaningful contribution to the peaceful resolution of whatever problems may confront the human race, so that we can set up a promising future for generations to come.

2

Teaching with Love

Who is the happiest of men? He who values the merits of others, and in their pleasure takes joy, even as though it were his own.

Johann von Goethe

Countless times over my 33-year teaching career I witnessed unhappy moments in the professional lives of faculty. Most complaints ranged from student disobedience to unfair treatment received from colleagues or the administration. Many such incidents kept reminding me that perhaps faculty members themselves attracted the treatment due to their approach to teaching. In this respect, it is possible that their views on the student-teacher relationship or that between faculty and the administration was marked by rigidity and a misunderstanding of who we really are in the larger scheme of things. Over time, I arrived at the conclusion that meaningless and egotistical confrontation leads to setting unnecessary distance between people. Indeed, it is ironical that some educators fail to realize that for a harmonious relationship between students and instructors, as well as among faculty, one should display acceptance, patience, understanding, cooperation, and awareness of imperfections, without sacrificing their own principles. Above all, if one can approach human encounters with unconditional love, most problems are solved before escalating. Consequently, I would like to share a few thoughts that might help teachers build an optimal educational environment.

Trust

Trust your students. In most cases people are honest. It is true that we have to allow for exceptions, but a well-thought saying suggests that usually "exceptions reinforce the rule." How true! We also have to remember that if people (students) are dishonest with us (instructors), sooner or later their act will be properly balanced and, more importantly, we don't have to do anything about it (I will treat this subject in more detail in a later essay where I will share a personal experience in Let the Universe Handle the Details). Such a trust will allow us to spend our positive energy on teaching, instead of chasing possibilities of deceit that might just be an exercise in futility.

Tolerance and Cooperation

Trust allows us to give the benefit of a doubt, which in return will reward us with a greater ability to tolerate apparent noncompliance with the set requirements. We need to remember that there are no laws that have never been broken. Indeed, if there were, then there is no need for such lows. Consequently, as teachers, we should use our own course requirements in a flexible way, a way that serves the student, without, of course, sacrificing the integrity of our teaching. Example: A student comes in with a valid excuse and requests to take a test late; within a reasonable timeframe, we should allow the student to take that test even if it flows a few days out of the lineup prescribed by the syllabus. In fact, such flexibility does not hurt anyone and it might just help students salvage a semester in which they really applied themselves. On the other hand, if the respective student is failing anyway, a little help from the instructor on these lines will most likely not alter the course of the semester for that student. However, it might just trigger a determination mechanism in students that will help them be successful the following semester.

Patience

It has been proverbially said that teachers display high levels of patience, and that is why, when I ask my students how many of them plan to become teachers, the common response is: "No. I have no patience to deal with unruly students!" To this, I occasionally answer, jokingly, "Good. That means I will have no competition 5-6 years from now!" And yes, it is true that teachers do need to show patience in a variety of classroom and office circumstances. However, this is a trait that can be acquired with proper pedagogical preparation and practice. As it takes patience to ensure a harmonious family environment, it takes even more patience to facilitate an amicable atmosphere among strangers in an educational institution. That is when the experience, expertise, and personality of the instructor become evident. In the end, patience can make or break the well-intended efforts toward success on behalf of both student and instructor.

Hug

Different cultures around the world have preserved over the centuries unique traditions in displaying human affection. Among these, a hand shake, a fist bump, a high-five, a lady's hand kiss, a cheek kiss (or two-three as is the case in Europe and the Middle East), are the best known. However, the one show of affection and unconditional love I treasure most is the hug. The actual embrace, as a display of caring for the other person, embodies that unmistakable ancestral feeling of closeness so vividly evidenced by a mother's hug of her beloved newborn. Nothing is as pure as that. And that is why, many years ago, I gradually adopted hugging as the pure choice of manifesting affection and care for the next person, including new contacts. I recommend it enthusiastically, especially in the field of education where it can break invisible barriers between teachers and students from the first day of school to the last. On this line, a good philosophical advice suggests that even when we meet people for the first time we should treat them as we have already known them; what a great way to instantly make new friends!

Humor

By humor I do not mean cruel sarcasm that can often offend people. The contrary is true. Humor should be used to lighten up the atmosphere, such that people could feel comfortable and encouraged to express themselves freely. This becomes paramount in the field of education. Not only do students feel more at home in the classroom, but it can also establish a positive and productive relationship between faculty members working closely together. After all, should we prefer the alternative? No. A cold and dry attitude as we engage others is doomed from the start to set invisible barriers between people. The paradigm of separation, still so prevalent in our modern society, can be in this way reinforced, and I don't think we should persist on that path. Details can be found in my 2007 *We Are All One* where I presented scientific, spiritual, and personal experience arguments for a paradigm of union versus one of separation.

Love

And, yes, love. Nothing compares with a compassionate smile of understanding as we attempt to help a student or a colleague with a problem. The display of concerned love is disarming. Rarely would anyone respond with hostility when we embrace them within a loving atmosphere. Indeed, many a time I had this happen in my office. Students or colleagues would come in with, sometimes, very serious problems, and in the privacy of a mutually accepted closed-door setting, we would share thoughts that ultimately would bring positive resolutions. I have had students at the brink of mental collapse feeling the need to talk to me as they were desperately searching for an escape from their apparent dead-end situation. Nevertheless, it helped. It seems that simply by focusing on love, patience, and understanding, people can draw out the solutions to their own problems with less effort than by confrontation; after all, as in mathematics, the solution is hidden in the problem.

Therefore, I hope that all of us instructors can build a more person-to-person philosophy of teaching. To substantially improve the quality of education, love, compassion, and affection should be incorporated in our teaching practice, since we are intrinsically connected with our students and colleagues in a web of human relationships that, true, sometimes escapes immediate scrutiny.

3

Personal Responsibility

*Always bear in mind that your own resolution to success is
more important than any other one thing.*

Abraham Lincoln

I started my *Teach For Life* volume with an essay
titled "Why Education?" in which I presented what I
consider the main purpose of education. Personal responsibility is an important part of that. Not only do
graduates at all academic levels need to set one more
brick in the wall of self-reliance as dependable human
beings, but they also must display high levels of responsibility. By this I mean to evolve to a place where
they take charge of their destiny without falling prey
to dependency or choosing to set blame for their short-
comings on others and the circumstances in their lives.
In this respect, I would like to suggest three major areas of responsibility we should have in mind: responsibility for self, responsibility for others, and
responsibility for the environment.

Many times people are constrained to make decisions that can affect the rest of their lives. Sometimes
taking risks in order to better one's life requires a great
deal of responsibility. As soon as people take responsibility for the outcome of such decisions, they are em-
powered to improve the situation as well as absolve

themselves of regrets. To empower themselves, they should try to prevent setting blame on others or on the circumstances. Indeed, a strong sense of personal responsibility can raise the level of individual happiness and contentment, and in return may allow people to help others wherever they go.

As we can see, it is all a matter of choices. The sooner people realize this, the more impact their decisions will have in their own lives as well as in the lives of others. It is obvious, therefore, that the building of personal responsibility should start early in the education process and it should continue throughout one's life. It is never too late to start.

In terms of improving personal responsibility in schools, I suggest that it should be built in the philosophy of teaching. All of us developed some of our most predominant traits during our education years and we nostalgically remember the instructors responsible. I do remember mine. Consequently, I would like to propose that each one of us, instructors, make the best of our opportunity to instill in our students a deep sense of responsibility as we guide them through a carefully selected academic curriculum.

At least in mathematics, it should start with homework. It is well known that individual practice is the number one factor for success in the study of mathematics. Students should be charged with the responsibility of completing their homework in a timely manner. However, substantial grades should not be awarded for homework since it is work done usually without instructor supervision. This simple strategy sets the preparation responsibility clearly on the student's shoulders and can be a very effective way to raise the student's readiness to take charge and choose to take responsibility in all walks of life. After all, the high rate of success registered by implementing this practice will be the confirmation for its validity and an incentive to approach all other endeavors responsibly.

A second area in education that can help students build a commendable sense of responsibility is their commitment to actually attend classes regularly. It is logical that missing a significant number of classes diminishes the chance to do well in a course. Therefore, students should be responsible for their attendance purely out of the conviction that this is a major contributor to academic success. In this respect, instructors should not reward students with grades only for good attendance and they should craft a captivating and productive plan for their classroom activity.

A third possibility to help students improve their personal responsibility is in the area of communication and cooperation in the process of learning. Students should not be forced to participate nor should they be punished for lack thereof. Instead, they should be convinced via the instructor's teaching skills and pedagogical expertise that good cooperation will dramatically increase their chances for success. By taking responsibility for their own success, students can train themselves to open up all channels of communication, whether among students or with instructors, to optimize the outcome of their education. In the end this is another trait that will help them throughout their lives.

Last but not least, responsibility for our natural environment is paramount. The environment is, after all, the sustainer of life on Earth. Education, more so than any other avenue, should be the most effective way to convince our fellow human beings all across the globe of the importance of preserving (pre-serving!) nature. Classroom well-organized instruction in any subject matter intrinsically offers opportunities for such educational pearls that will help mold strong characters as far as caring for the environment is concerned.

Choosing to take responsibility rather than blaming others or external conditions is likely to empower the student. Consequently, all academic institutions should employ those strategies that help students develop a strong sense of personal responsibility. The obvious result is that graduates will become pillars of trust and examples of rational risk-takers that will help the entire society. After all, this is the ultimate goal of a respectable system of education dedicated to ensuring a better future for the human race.

4

Teach Excellence

When you reach for the stars, you may not quite get one, but you won't come up with a handful of mud, either.

Leo Burnett

A great saying suggests that the problem with human beings is not that we set our goals too high and we don't reach them, but that we set our goals too low and we do! I think there is a lot of truth to this, and in the following I will cluster my arguments for teaching excellence around this saying.

Many times I have students come to my office to ask what grade they should make on the final exam to pass the course. Invariably I answer: 100! To this they argue that according to their present average and the grading scheme, 100 seems to be too high. I respond: "Yes, you are right, but let's say you actually only need a 75; if you set your goal at 75 and you don't reach it, you fail, but if you set your goal at 100, working hard to accomplish it, even if you get a 90 or an 80 or even a 75, you pass. So, isn't it better to set your goal higher than the minimum necessary?" Most of the time students agree, and consequently, they push themselves harder to reach higher goals. On this line there is another educational truth: the more we ask our students to learn the more they will learn. They might not learn everything we ask them to know but the same kind of ratio applies even when we ask them to learn less. It is implicitly true then that asking for more, students do learn more than asking for less. Therefore, the road to excellence in education is setting higher standards under professionally delivered teaching. Unfortunately, some faculty entertain the false premise that asking for less gives students more time to learn it better.

Isn't this, though, common sense? Shouldn't we all set our goals high enough that their realization will challenge us to bring out the best in ourselves? I think we should. The alternative is to be content with less. Although choosing to be content with less may be appropriate in many other circumstances, in the world of education, this is a clear invitation to mediocrity and survival but not to excellence. Nothing of significance has been created in this world unless the creators were seeking the best they could provide. In this respect, competition among ideas is on the top of the list when it comes to the next step. For example, in science and medicine, discoveries are aimed at the best ways of improving the quality of human life; as rewards, the famous Nobel Price comes to mind, and we need to remember that funds are distributed according to results. Down to Earth, here are a few trades that illustrate well the need for teaching excellence: Automechanics (you would not have your car fixed by an average mechanic), builders (you wouldn't buy your house built under the required standards), medicine (you would not want to be treated by a mediocre doctor), computer programmers and software designers (you would not hire computer professionals with only average preparation, experience, and expertise), and, finally, education (you would employ the best teachers available, and we are all familiar with the selection process involved in the search for excellent instructors).

It seems obvious, therefore, that competition can be the engine that drives people to excellence, and this includes competition with oneself: become a better you today than you were yesterday. People also need to have well-defined incentives in order to rise from stagnation; incentives boost motivation in any endeavor and this includes education. After all, most college students are in college in order to improve themselves as they aspire to a prosperous life. To support these statements, I will elaborate on a few more examples from different areas of life including education.

Sports

And when I say sports I mean all sports and at all levels. Of course it is obvious that professional athletes, trainers, and coaches are all seeking excellence, hence winning: this is their profession. Not only that, but otherwise they will not survive in the world of competition, and the rewards are worth the effort (I experienced it first hand: I used to be a semiprofessional volleyball player; details are included in my autobiography *Escape to Freedom*). Also, think of the Olympics. So many success stories spring from this awesome two-thousand-year-old athletics tradition and this is not only in terms of setting records. Indeed, many participants had to compete with others and with themselves in order to qualify for Olympics. That means excellence; mediocrity not allowed. Many such athletes are or will turn professional as they get better than they were before. As in all life endeavors, making a good living on what you love doing is among the highest levels of achievement. On the other hand, take the recreational tennis players who simply want to improve; it is still a competition with themselves but a competition for excellence nevertheless, at their own levels.

Arts

Let us look at the movie business. A motion picture competes with many others on a tough international market of talented movie makers. From the theme, to the script, to the producers, directors and actors, each is in competition for excellence. Of course not all final products are reaching the highest level, but we can bet that all are trying. And in the end that is what it's all about: attempt your best. Beside movies, all other art forms are subject to the same criteria for success: music makers, painters, writers, sculptors, or designers are all in the same game of producing excellence. A friend of mine, a professional concert pianist, mind you, once said (while giving piano lessons) that she was against piano competitions; I quickly responded: "How would you have become so good if not for competing with others and with yourself as you were seeking excellence?"

Business

By it, I mean business in the free world of commerce. Of course this becomes the optimum domain of competition toward reaching excellence. Companies producing the same or similar goods must compete with others as far as quality and price are concerned. Excellence is, therefore, paramount. Excellence in organization, excellence in preparation, excellence in recruiting the proper personnel, and excellence in delivery will ensure success in the long run. The product quality and flexibility on pricing are natural outcomes of excellence throughout the free enterprise system, of course in compliance with the applicable legislation. Mediocrity has no place in this as long as the aim is full success and not just survival. The aim for excellence emerges once again, as any respectable business should avoid mediocrity at all costs.

Politics

Should I say more? The world of politics in democratic societies portrays one of the best examples of the need for excellence in the pursuit of victory. Only excellent political teams win elections. Of course, this is so since voters are not stupid. People recognize quality, and quality comes from excellence. One could debate motives and political orientations but only excellence in organization and strategy of a political campaign can win in the end.

Education

Yes, finally, education. I left it last because it is obvious to me that it is at the core of any other example of excellence. Indeed, in order to be excellent in anything one must be excellently educated (trained) in that particular field. There are only a few exceptions as some astonishing feats are accomplished by mediocre performers. In order to secure the best chances of consistent success, one should first focus on preparation. A mediocre preparation (education) can only pave the road to mediocrity. My conclusion is, therefore, that education, from K to Ph.D., should strive for excellence at every step on this road. But excellence in education implies excellent educators. However, we are caught in a vicious circle here: most educators are produced in the same system of education in which they would eventually perform. It logically follows, therefore, that if a system of education is not competitive internationally, it will be almost impossible to improve, left only to its own resources. That is when 'imports' should take place. Tested ideas and fresh blood from abroad should be gradually assimilated in order to amend the old. As an example, I will consider the teaching of mathematics in the U.S. Striving for excellence should open the door to better successful approaches and curriculum design, remote from a strategy diligently fed only or in large part by technology that encourages a limited learning of mathematics. Excellence in the study of mathematics means to actually know and understand it, not to know only something about it – details are provided in other essays included herein and in my volume *Teach For Life*.

5

Teacher Education Requirements

The man who has done his level best, and who is conscious that he has done his best, is a success, even though the world may write him down a failure.

B.C. Forbes

As I compare educational systems from other countries to that of the U.S.A., I find that there is a striking difference in what concerns the preparation of teachers and instructors at most academic levels. In this respect, I will describe my findings, considering my 33 years of first-hand experience with the U.S. secondary and college education in mathematics, and I will assess how this fairs internationally.

Notable is the fact that in international math contests at the secondary level, the U.S. is not placing as high as expected. On one hand, this can be justified by a difference in curriculum, since the minimum requirements for a high school diploma are significantly lower in the U.S. than most other countries. On the other hand, we could also consider the preparation of educators: the general teaching preparation requirement for secondary education instructors in many other nations is a master's degree, while in the U.S. only a bachelor degree is required. As we compare these two realities, we can easily understand that there is room for improvement in the U.S. secondary education at least with respect to the curriculum and the professional readiness of the instructors in the classroom.

Nowhere is this more visible than in the first years of college and in the role of the two-year higher education institutions, mainly the community colleges. Indeed, statistical evidence is overwhelming: a large percentage of students entering college are in stringent need of remediation in mathematics. It is obvious that the secondary math preparation is not set at the desired college-ready standard. That is where remedial (developmental) college programs come into play in order to complete students' math background, knowledge and skills they should have received in high school.

It seems, therefore, that 12 years of pre-college education is not always producing college-ready graduates. In search of a solution to such a situation, we must return to the above-described two possible causes: the pre-college curriculum and the teacher preparation. While curriculum can be easily amended with the proper attention of the academic decision-making boards, a more sensitive problem appears to be that of enhancing the professionalism of the educators.

In this respect, one relatively simple solution is to make the master's degree a requirement for high school teachers of mathematics. Not only will this ensure more knowledgeable instructors in the classroom, but through a more thorough student preparation, it will also close the gap between high school and college. Such an improvement will be significant for the student.

However, as far as the U.S. higher education is concerned, we witness a further deficiency in the teaching of mathematics mainly in four-year colleges and universities. Apparently pressed by financial constraints, many such institutions don't hire professional assistant instructors in the classroom, but instead they employ their own inexperienced graduate students at a much lower pay. Since most of these are research universities, the fulltime professor assigned to teach is rarely seen in the classroom, while the graduate student (the 'assistant instructor') is teaching the course. One should wonder, therefore, about the quality of mathematics instruction provided this way to large groups of undergraduates. In parallel, most respected institutions of higher education abroad take more pride in the delivery of education by hiring experienced professional assistant instructors. Moreover, the professor assigned to teach, honors her/his responsibility in the classroom, while the assistant fulfills all the other duties. We can see, then, that students are better served in a system where education is delivered in the most professional way, placing high esteem on student academic preparation.

The conclusion is obvious. In order to provide our students optimal education, the pre-college curriculum needs to be drastically amended to be internationally compatible, while the teaching requirements for high school mathematics instructors should be raised from bachelors to master's. Finally, as a necessary improvement in higher education, math courses should not be taught by inexperienced graduate students but by the full professors assigned to teach, while their research duties should be fulfilled over the remainder of the time of their contracts.

6

Basic Skills in Mathematics

Start by doing what's necessary, then what's possible, and suddenly you are doing the impossible.
Saint Francis of Assisi

The Use of Calculators

Let me start with the problem of calculators in basic math. Yes, this issue should belong more to the philosophy of education than just to the teaching of a math course. As instructors, we are here for our students and we should impart all we know, of course accepting the fact that we are constrained by the subject matter and the time we have available. We can teach any math course in a variety of ways: some approaches offer immediate "positive" results but some offer life-long skills, like number sense! A good number sense (a sense of numbers as we refer to addition, subtraction, multiplication, and division) is indispensable in all walks of life, especially for nurses, doctors, engineers, financial experts, or simply for doing your own bookkeeping and taxes, and estimating discounts on the spot as well as evaluating products, prices and sales in a grocery store. In this respect, it is well known that extensive use of calculators, especially at the developmental level, precludes students from developing a good number sense. I think it is bad enough that many high school districts allow wide use of calculators; colleges, especially community colleges, should correct this educational error instead of deepening it!

After all, most of us, math instructors, have completed our higher education with very little or no use of calculators; consequently, we have a good number sense. It seems highly hypocritical for math educators at any level to encourage extensive use of calculators: we should desire that our students gain more mathematical ability not less than we have. We really want future generations to live up to their complete potential, versus being dependent on some electronic gadget at all times. It is truly sad to see students in intermediate algebra and beyond reaching for a calculator to divide 72 by 2, to say that 7 times 8 is 54, or not being able to evaluate 10% of 140 in 2 seconds mentally! In fact there are many situations when a good number sense helps one do calculations faster than with a calculator, as we all know. After all, if you could change channels on your TV set with your mind would you use a remote control?

Moreover, once students master and understand well a math concept using the power of their mind, it is easier, faster, and more comfortable to learn to use a piece of technology. From the point of view of mathematics, by allowing students to not understand why, what, and how things work behind the screen of a calculator or computer is one of the most detrimental educational practices conceivable. Basic math operations must be understood not only performed. The question why should be on the lips of the instructors and students all the time. Only asking how and what but not why, promotes a mechanical learning and we all agree that we, and our students, are human beings not machines.

As responsible human beings, we, community college faculty attempt to re-teach in three short semesters 12 years of mathematics that for many of our students are largely missing! In this respect, do we really think that using calculators in basic math is the best practice?

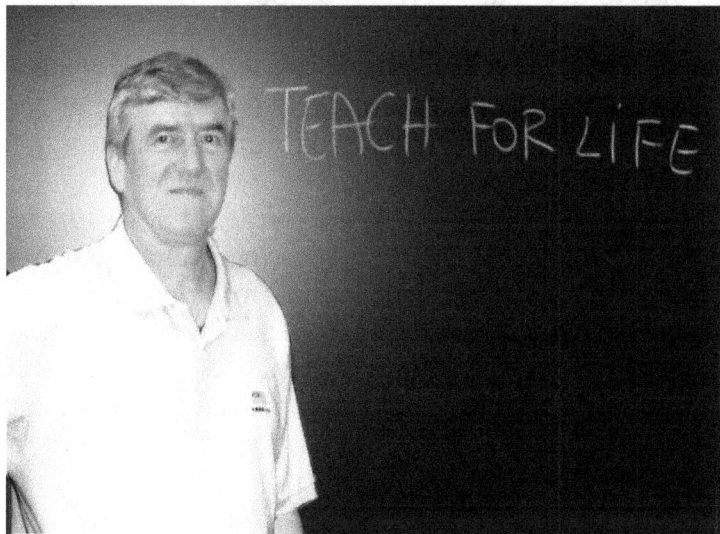

Irie Glajar in the Classroom

We need to remember that, in math education, completing tasks by hand and in our minds is also very good training for organized thinking, for memorization (which is strictly necessary in many cases), and for rational analysis within a logical context. Also from a biological perspective, multiplying 12 by 11 mentally, for example, closes more neuronal circuits than using a calculator. Implementing mental processes is known to be very beneficial to the human being as a whole entity at any age!

In addition, and contrary to popular belief, it is not that difficult to develop a good number sense: all that students need is practice and repetition on the multi-plication table, addition, subtraction, and division with numbers less than 100, enhanced by common sense numerical strategies. Of course this extends to fractions, finding common denominators, factoring numbers, and also to decimals, percent, proportions, slopes, inequalities, etc. But this is not going to happen over only a semester or two. Therefore, the traditional three developmental math courses at a community college, for example, should help set a good number sense foundation for all our students.

However, allowing and encouraging widespread use of calculators in mathematics in general, just because they are available, is putting millions of dollars in the pockets of the manufacturers as we undermine the process of real learning. The "new trends" and the "21st century" attitude are not proven to be better teaching strategies; they are just fashionable under a strong high-tech financial gain push! Education systems in Europe and Asia, well known for their good teaching of math and sciences, rely much less on the use of calculators and computers. Results in secondary education international competitions in these fields are illustrative: unfortunately, the U. S. doesn't place very high.

Even though many faculty members are infatuated with technology, forcing or allowing students to spend even more hours on screens stops or at least diminishes their independent thinking. There are books and articles written on this subject, and the high-tech dependency already manifested in our society is truly scary; the problem is even more sensitive in mathematics education. Lacking a good number sense, one often cannot tell whether the answer from a calculator is right or wrong: what if they punched the wrong key or misplaced the decimal point?

Therefore, we need to carefully reconsider the way we approach this subject and to have in mind the long-term implication: our students should develop into independent thinkers, responsible, innovative, and creative human beings. As we ask them to learn more, they will learn more – perhaps not everything we ask them to, but definitely more than the minimum they will learn otherwise. Mathematics education should not be just about meeting some fuzzy "course objectives" and fitting into some "projected outcomes," since human beings are much more than statistics.

With this goal in mind I propose that calculators should not be allowed at the basic math level, and their use should be very limited over the rest of the developmental sequence. Indeed, at least at this level all math concepts can be very well mastered with the power of the human mind alone. I regularly survey my students in developmental classes, and a majority agree that calculators are not necessary and that they are even detrimental. Some students write "thank you" notes later for having the opportunity to improve their number sense that helped them substantially in subsequent courses and in their life experiences.

Course redesign

As with most stories, there are at least two sides to the acclaimed 'course redesign' makeover of developmental math courses at community colleges. After I closely inspected the "Summary of Major Aspects" of course redesign, I am happy to notice that the instructor is still allowed to partially teach the course, but then the problems start.

They start due to a major online component of this design. First, online assessments are unsupervised. Since these assignments carry 30% of the final grade, it can mean significant grade inflation, as well as an easier reaching of the "projected outcome," which automatically leads to a false higher success rate. Second, even at the most basic level of developmental mathematics there are many students who don't need the so called "online reading quizzes." For example: why should they be forced to read the section and take the quiz before class when they can do very well without this extra time-consuming work? There is a substantial possibility that many students will lose the novelty and the curiosity offered by the class session since the instructor is more or less repeating what they read prior to class. The sense of participation in the process of thinking out the solution to a new problem may be lost, so the class presentation can become very boring! What can the instructor do then to keep class interesting and captivating? Third, many students do not need to do the entire "online homework" list all the time. Then, why should they be penalized with low "online homework" grades when they can do well without this extra pressure, especially when talking about enforced "strict due dates?" Fourth, "weekly in-class quizzes" focused only on mathematical notations are given too much weight (20% of the final grade!). In the end, the real diagnostic on what the students know is based only 50% on supervised tests and the final exam over the course content! Consequently, proponents of 'course redesign' actually make a false claim of success which is largely based on grade inflation.

As far as the summary of "Benefits of the Course Redesign" is concerned, in light of the previous considerations, I don't see many. Technology should be used at a minimum, if at all. Many students display obvious distress toward online math work – early in the semester some request to be transferred to instructors (courses) that don't use the online approach. Then, can we really talk about "consistency of content and instruction" since instructors who teach in the traditional format have the flexibility of teaching the course in class without the 'aid' of online work? Just because students are forced to do "consistently" all the same things online is not necessarily a constructive pedagogical approach in this age when we value multiple intelligences and learning styles!

And now comes a sensitive component of course redesign, namely "student self-directed study." As we want to increase student responsibility for their education, imposing strict deadlines and rigid modalities to complete tasks is not the optimal way to go. Such an approach sounds more like a dictatorial strategy: do this, or else! Many students, many times don't need to do all of the work 'required.' We should provide solid instruction in class, assign homework, offer office hours and tutoring lab availability at flexible times each day, 7 days a week (and we do), so that students should exercise responsibility to choose or not, any of the available help at their convenience. Of course we do need to implement a flexible time table as we have in mind the complexity of college students' lives - work, family, transportation, taking other courses - and we should not punish them by imposing a super-rigid educational regimen. When students can pass or fail a class based on 30% credit for online work (plus "notation" quizzes) forced on them regardless of their performance on the supervised tests, quizzes, and the final exam, the determination of the correct grades becomes even more speculative.

In this respect, true progress can be easily tracked and documented by having content quizzes, tests, attendance, direct eye-to-eye contact between instructor and student in and out of class throughout the semester. There is no need for any required digital and impersonal intermediary.

Consequently, "course redesign," although well intended, seems to be a financially and politically driven attempt at solving a non-existing problem in math education. Displaying the usefulness and the beauty of mathematics should be done by qualified instructors in person, with the students, but not by imposing some "one-size-fits-all" tinted approach to education, approach already proven unproductive around the world in all walks of life.

Finally, it becomes obvious that, for the sake of education and our students, the use of calculators and software in developmental mathematics should be left optional at best, if not entirely eliminated except for extreme situations. Technology evolves at a rapid pace and becomes significantly simpler and easier to use as time passes. This, if it wants to survive! When students can do mathematics by hand and in their mind, learning to use a piece of technology, even in the field of work after graduation, should be easy and fast: "even a caveman could do it," as the saying goes. To prematurely use such technology, before learning the reasoning, logic, and theory involved in how to handle the task, could lead to a resurgence of caveman intelligence.

7

Grades and Grading

Life becomes harder for us when we live for others, but it also becomes richer and happier.

Albert Schweitzer

Let me start by saying that grades should reflect what each student knows in the respective subject matter. To accomplish such a sensitive and important goal, instructors should use a grading scheme that assesses knowledge, with little emphasis on participation, attendance, work done without supervision, etc. At the same time, we need to keep in mind that grading is only relatively accurate in measuring a student's readiness, which is one more reason to give grading much attention and fairness.

In general, we grade on a scale from 0 to 100, considering grades over 70 as passing grades. Interpreting these as percent, students need to score 70% or better to pass a course. In order to identify the level of mastery by a student, we also establish letter grades denoting in general an A for 90% to 100%, a B for 80% to 89%, a C for 70% to 79%, a D for 60% to 69%, and F for grades less than a 60%. One can easily see how relative this scale can be. The question is: where do we draw the line between a C and a D, for example, which means between passing or not passing a course. The reality is that some instructors are more rigid than others, and this seems to be unfair to many students.

In this respect, we need to remember that a letter grade spreads over ten percentage points. At least in mathematics, the final grade is the average of grades earned over an entire semester. Although the grading criteria vary, in general grades are based on quizzes, tests, homework, participation, and final exams. With such a wide range of very different evaluation tools, and considering also partial credit given in many situations, it seems very reasonable to know that there is a certain level of subjectivity in all grading. Therefore, a ten-point spread of a letter grade is a pretty wide range to classify the academic readiness of a student especially when it comes down to passing or failing.

As we strive for fairness in grading, in light of the grading system described above, we need to examine and improve our practice. True stories of attributing final grades reveal 'drastic' approaches based seemingly on an overly rigid implementation of the classical scale. What is a 90%: an A or a B? Many of us instructors would consider an 89.5% an A, but some do not, which I find very unreasonable. As we consider the vast grading scale and the ten-point range of one letter grade, it seems much more logical to round up decimal grades instead of rounding down. Besides that, it becomes more important for the student since a final grade can decide between pass and fail.

Considering the periodic quiz and test grades throughout the semester, I would suggest an even more flexible approach: use the supper-market prices model. The strategy of setting prices seems to be based on the 'first digit impression' since that is a factor to which we pay more attention: a $4.95 'looks' better than $5, although the actual difference is almost insignificant. The motivation for such an approach, I think, is to make the clients feel better, believing they get a good deal. Similarly, if we arrive at a fairly consistent periodic grade of a 69% during the semester, for example, probably we should not round it up to a 70% since the motivation effect to do better on the next examination is most likely enhanced by the lower grade, while in effect the difference is small. Such a strategy is not really hurting the student and, as we consider the difference between a C and a B or between a B and an A, it might represent the boost some students need to strive for excellence instead of being content with mediocrity. However, we should reserve the right to round up especially as nearly passing final grades are concerned.

In the end, the entire grading procedure, more so when we grant partial credit, is relative. Since an A as a letter grade on the transcript of a student could be actually anything between 90% and a 100%, the difference is actually ignored in the long run. Consequently, it makes little sense to stumble over a half of a one percent, even more so when we decide the final grade; rounding up is therefore more logical when it can help a student pass a course.

In light of all of this, we need to remember that as instructors we carve a long-term mark on our students' records and self-esteem. In spite of some random negative stories we might hear, students do appreciate fairness in grading and most of them are responsive to our encouragement and consideration. Not only will such an attitude help them in the present, but it will establish a positive pattern in their lives, able to see that their efforts are rewarded as they aspire to a better future.

8

Departmental Math Exams

Every man is said to have his peculiar ambition.

Abraham Lincoln

Some mathematics departments embrace the practice of designing departmental exams or at least departmental final exams. To accomplish this, a group of faculty members work together in crafting what they consider a proper exam for all students in a certain course of study at the respective institution. While national universal assessment tests do serve a purpose even as "one test fits all," I think the story is drastically different when it comes to individual courses at a particular academic institution.

The teaching of mathematics is a very complex matter as math instructors do the best they can to prepare students for subsequent courses and to provide the final mathematics experience before they graduate. But just learning the mathematics is not enough. Education is vastly more than acquiring skills to perform a task, and this applies abundantly to mathematics. Education should help graduates become harmonious and flexible thinkers able to adjust, improvise, and create solutions on the job. Mathematics does just that: teaches one to think in a well-organized sequence of logical steps within a reasoning strategy. For this, experienced instructors should be allowed to exercise their discretion as far as the structure of the daily teaching activity is concerned. The manner of testing students should also be left as one of their main priorities.

However, this is not the case at institutions that employ departmental testing in mathematics. In a way, such practice is insulting to the instructor. It is akin to saying: "We trust you to teach the course for an entire semester, but when it comes to the final exam we don't think you are competent enough to design a good one." Ironically, since finals are graded only by the respective instructor it mercifully defeats the purpose of a departmental exam. And there are several other crucial problems with respect to departmental testing in mathematics.

Most departments that impose a departmental final exam also give out a "Review for the final exam" a few weeks before the administration of the exam. This practice is very close to a widely accepted no-no in the teaching of mathematics at any level: teaching to the test. Indeed, since the actual final exam is just a shorter version of the review, with, of course different numerical values, but identical kinds of questions, the problem is evident. It is a clear sacrifice, therefore, of the flexibility, diversity, and even academic freedom with which every instructor should be entrusted. In the meantime, students may be deprived of being tested on their ability to apply a learned skill to other factual situations that some instructors might choose to explore.

Another significant problem with departmental exams is that of security. Since such exams may be little changed from semester to semester, there is a heavy reliance on the department relative to their security. It is true that if a student were to possess a copy of the exam, students who would take the same course in the subsequent semester could have a very clear idea of what to expect on the final. Consequently, departmental exams are administered under the close supervision of the instructor and graded exams are never given back to students; inquiring students can see their exams in the instructor's office but would not be allowed to keep them.

We should also be concerned about mathematics departmental exams from a pedagogical point of view. This springs directly from the fact that students are not allowed to get back and keep their departmental final exams. Since math finals are meant to present an overall picture of course mastery, students would have much to learn from their mistakes, hence they should be able to keep their finals and use them for future reference. Such practice will not only allow students to fully understand their final grade in the course, but will help them be better prepared for the next step in their mathematics education, which in the end should be the chief priority of any mathematics department. In this respect, departmental math finals may well be more harmful than departmental exams in other areas of education.

The alternative to departmental final exams in math is therefore obviously far better: instructors should design brand new finals every semester, grade them, and students should be allowed to keep them. Not only would this help students learn from their mistakes as they receive back their finals, but it would also help instructors take full charge of their teaching. Yes, perhaps the department (the respective course committee) should collect a copy of every instructor's final exam in order to ensure consistency across the department, but instructors should be in charge of their own finals. As professionals, they should create meaningful exams in accord with their specific student population, which is in fact a major purpose of any course. Their choices and preferences as to math concepts selection should be honored. Once the department collects samples of the finals from all instructors, others can benefit from a wide variety of exams, which can be a valuable source of inspiration. In conclusion, allowing instructors the freedom to create their own final exams anew every semester will eliminate the 'security' issue, it will increase the instructor's direct involvement in the decision-making process, and, most importantly, it will offer students yet another avenue to improve their learning.

9

Abuse of Technology

I am afraid a day will come when technology will overcome humanity; only a generation of idiots will be left in the world.

Albert Einstein

A careful look around us, at home, on the sidewalk, in the park, in the store, in the hallways and classrooms of educational institutions, and at virtually any place of employment, reveals that a majority of people literally live on a screen. Indeed, in an effort to stay 'connected' people are constantly on a cell phone. To do their basic calculations – including school – people use pocket calculators. To stay on top of the news, for their favored entertainment, and to keep up with the most recent releases in the motion picture industry they spend countless hours in front of a television set or a personal computer. People are less frequently visiting the old fashion 'big screen' at the cinema. Moreover, an increasing number of people favor shopping online instead of visiting the stores.

We can see, then, how dependent on technology modern society in the developed world has become. Under such circumstances, it is obvious that the direct human-to-human contact is neglected, which has negative implications on a large scale. Not only do people lose their ability to interact with others face to face in order to solve ordinary problems, but they also impart this deficiency to future generations by creating long-lasting dependency on technology. To top off this entire scenario, I cannot even imagine what would happen in case electricity ceases. Virtually all technology functions on electricity. If one could deliberately 'turn it off,' most of the human race would be terminally paralyzed due to the self-chosen and self-created dependency on electrical technological gadgets.

As we examine the school environment at any academic level, we witness this trend expanding at an alarming rate. From the youngest ages, children are set in front of screens playing video games and 'educational' videos. Such a practice prevents children from physically playing with children, from socializing with others in the direct and tangible real world, thereby limiting the understanding of what it means to be human. As children become adolescents in secondary school and then adults in higher education, the trend is perpetuated by an educational system which is more and more sold to the idea that computers are indispensable in education.

At least in the area of mathematics this is almost completely untrue (exceptions should be granted but only in special situations). To outsource the teaching of mathematics to a piece of software could be the most offensive affront to a professional mathematics teacher. Not only that, but a preprogrammed mechanical methodology of teaching mathematics cannot, by any means, accomplish all that a pedagogically trained human being can lively do in the classroom. However, not to overlap contents in the essays of this collection, please refer to others on the theme of mathematics education and implementation of technology.

So, as we can see, once again Albert Einstein seems to be right. We do have to take careful precaution in terms of accepting this scenario: as useful and convenient technology might be at times, we should not let ourselves be taken by it; otherwise, it will almost certainly mean a radical and potentially fatal downfall to the human race as we know it. Consequently, we should strive to strike a lucrative and reasonable balance between the use of technology and the preservation of natural human activities, abilities and talents in teaching and learning. This balance can be sought in the spirit of saving some of our most sensitive and important traits: emotions, sensitivity, compassion, patience, understanding, inspiration, and, why not, sensible intelligence.

10

Misdirected Funding in U.S. Education

So what do we do? Anything. Something. So long as we just don't sit there. If we screw it up, start over. Try something else. If we wait until we've satisfied all the uncertainties, it may be too late.

Lee Iacocca

January 25th, 1982 was the day I first stepped foot on American soil at New York's LaGuardia Airport at the end of a trans-Atlantic flight from Rome, Italy. After securing a Master's degree in mathematics and computer science upon my 1979 graduation in Romania, and after my stay in a political refugee camp in Italy, via the American embassy in Rome, I received my green card as a permanent resident of the United States of America. At the end of a fortunate job search, in August, 1982 I started teaching mathematics in a private high school in Austin, Texas (details are available in my autobiography *Escape to Freedom*).

Beginning with the fall semester of 1982, I taught high school mathematics for 12 years, while since 1984 I have been earning my college teaching experience as an adjunct faculty member at Austin Community College (ACC). For the spring semester of 1994 I was selected as a full time mathematics instructor at ACC (out of almost 90 applicants) where I have enjoyed teaching ever since. Worth mentioning, perhaps, is that from 1994 to 1997, that position also entailed developmental math departmental chair duties. In parallel, from 1999 to 2002 I also taught undergraduate mathematics as a visiting lecturer at The University of Texas at Austin. In the meantime, since 1994, I have been attending countless academic conferences and workshops not only across the U.S.A. but also in Canada and Romania.

In light of my academic experience, therefore, I can say that one major problem with the public elementary, secondary, and college undergraduate education in the United States is funding. By this I don't mean that there is a lack of funds. No. What I would like to emphasize is that much of the available funds seem to be misused, misdirected, and in fact wasted on unproductive and even detrimental avenues as far as a solid academic education is concerned.

What do I mean by this? Over my 12-year tenure of teaching high school mathematics in two private Austin institutions, I repeatedly faced the reality behind what we term 'policies of public education.' Versus private institutions, many public schools use more funds per student to produce lesser results. It is a known fact that in an overwhelming majority of cases, (at least in the U.S. high schools) private education is better and cheaper than its counterpart, the public education. Why? It seems that rules and regulations imposed from above in a complex net of bureaucracies, combined with public pressure to spend more in hope of better outcomes, are at the foundation of this discrepancy. Indeed, when people are directly involved in the process they immediately fund, they feel more responsible for the outcomes, and therefore, they are more personally involved in demanding optimal results from their investment. That is exactly what I felt for all of the 12 years of my teaching in private high schools: direct responsibility; not only on behalf of the parents of our students, but implicitly on ourselves (teachers) as we were serving our institutions.

Within this scenario, it seems we sometimes forget that people are people, and people are not perfect. As far as public education is concerned, deep in the higher administration ranks (let that be at state and federal levels), people decide according to their ability and to their interests. Consequently, funds are channeled into directions that often don't serve the real academic interest of students, and the results are disastrous.

We witness such results daily. My 32-year experience at the community college level in mathematics education underlines a clear fact. As they apply to college, instead of placing in college credit courses, many high school graduates place into developmental math, reading, or writing, which means that they have to complete first at least some of the standard remediation courses offered by community colleges. Why? The answer is simple: they did not receive the proper education in high school (mathematics is the best candidate for this argument). But this screams for yet another explanation: why, when they spend more than most private schools per student, don't public secondary educational institutions adequately prepare their students? Besides low academic standards, the other strong reason I find is that the funds are misdirected, as I mentioned before. Instead of focusing on the direct process of education, instead of hiring well-prepared faculty (even raising the academic preparation requirements for their faculty or retraining efforts), secondary education institutions spend a bulk of their available funds elsewhere, heavy bureaucracy, to name one area.

Where else? What is so important in the process of secondary education that funds must be shifted in that direction? Or, a better question: are there really more significant areas in which public money should be invested? Apparently some public secondary education employees in charge have found them: athletics, for example. However, as much as I treasure sports, this should not be a number one priority. To cut arts and language programs in favor of excessive athletics sends a wrong cultural message to the entire society; it suggests that we value more cheerleading and rivalry athletics competition, and we care less about culture. Such a policy might temporarily feed some egos, but in the long run it becomes a societal calamity.

And there is more than bureaucracy and athletics. Recent times expose another dangerous development that unfortunately many educators support. This can be even more damaging to the process of thorough education since it is well camouflaged under the euphoria of and the addiction to new gadgets in education, namely electronic technology. At least in undergraduate mathematics education, I am convinced that far too much credit is being given to online teaching and calculator/software dependency, as new generations of math instructors (at all academic levels) seem to embrace such approaches. Not only are these new trends pedagogically unsound, they also impose a huge financial burden on educational institutions and implicitly on students. Publishers pre-pack mathematics textbooks together with pertinent software that raises the price sometimes nearly to two hundred dollars per individual. Especially at a community college level, where many students are struggling financially, such prices are obviously a significant burden.

Closely connected is the issue of hardware. Institutions find themselves under the pressure of 'keeping up with the times' so to speak, and they invest dangerously high amounts of money in computers whether they are necessary or not. High schools and colleges dress multiple computer labs with the so called 'state of the art' technology that, at least in mathematics, is really setting an artificial intermediary between students' minds and thinking and the natural process of learning delivered by a well-prepared teacher in the classroom. While instructors in such labs are still 'in charge' of the course of study and therefore paid, there is suddenly an additional and not a modest cost: expensive computers, expensively equipped computer labs that inflict huge amounts of electricity consumption, and computer experts as lab assistants. Once again, undergraduate mathematics teaching does not require such a departure from the traditional approach. A well-written textbook (and most of them are) that includes well-thought-out homework sets of practice problems is *all* students need to rigorously learn mathematics, provided they have an experienced and dedicated instructor in the classroom. No extra expenditure is needed, regardless of new trends and the financially motivated push into exclusive use of technology. We need to remember that not all new trends in education are necessarily good and constructive. If we still treasure quality, depth, and thoroughness in the teaching of mathematics, for the sake of many future generations of graduates, we should slow down dramatically the handing of education to artificial means of delivery.

Consequently, based on my long-term experience as a mathematics instructor, I suggest that one possible avenue to improve undergraduate education is to re-examine the distribution of funds. A wiser selection of educational areas in need of more funds would definitely assure the progress to which we all aspire in teaching and learning. In this respect, I hope those in charge of directing available funds would approach their responsibility with great care, such that waste is limited and investments take the U.S. education to the next level as it is trying to compete globally.

11

Interview with Mrs. Ligia Darau

The direction in which education starts a man will determine his future in life.

Plato

In order to present some important aspects of the teaching of mathematics at the secondary level abroad, I include here an interview with Mrs. Ligia Darau, mathematics professor in Romania.

Mrs. Ligia Darau

Irie Glajar: Mrs. Darau, thank you very much for accepting to do this email interview. Please describe the institution and your position as a mathematics professor.

Ligia Darau: Thanks for inviting me, and I appreciate it. The institution is Colegiul Tehnic "Dr. A. Barbat" from Victoria, District of Brasov, Romania. Here we offer a full 9-12th grade high school program, 11-13th grade evening classes, 9-11th grade trade school, public food service training, and a 2-year post high school evening program. My position is that of a mathematics professor and department chair, and I teach day classes. I am also the 10th grade advisor, and I am a member of several committies, such as the scholarship committee, the committee in charge of verification of school documents, and the discipline committee.

IG: Please describe briefly the required academic preparation set by the Romanian Ministry of Education for your teaching position before the 1989 Romanian anti-communist Revolution and after.

LD: Before 1989 the requirement was the 4-year Diploma de Licenta in mathematics offered by state universities in a 2-step higher education system: Licenta and Doctorate. A few years after 1989 the requirement changed to a 3-year Diploma de Licenta followed by a 2-year Master's, due to the new 3-step higher education format meant to align the Romanian system to that of the European Union – Diploma de Licenta, Master's, and Doctorate.

IG: Please describe the academic level in mathematics of the students entering the 9th grade at your institution.

LD: Our 9th grade students are required to have covered from 5th through 8th grade the following: *arithmetic and algebra* (operations with real numbers, exponents, order of operations, sets and operations with sets, fractions, proportions, first and second degree equations, first degree inequalities, systems of equations of the first degree, algebraic simplifications including special products, first degree functions and graphs), and <u>geometry</u> (lines, angles, polygons, circles, units of measure, transformations, congruency and similarity of triangles, triangle properties, relations in the right triangle, Thales Theorem, Pythagorean Theorem, trigonometric relationships, points-lines-planes relationships, orthogonal projections on a plane, areas and volumes of three-dimensional solids).

IG: Please describe the academic level in mathematics of the 12th grade graduates as they apply to higher education institutions in Romania.

LD: Only the 12th grade graduates who passed the Baccalaureate examination can apply to universities. These students need to master the following: <u>algebra</u> (logics, arithmetic and geometric progressions, first and second degree functions, equations and inequalities, first and second degree systems of equations and inequalities, powers and radicals, the exponential and logarithmic functions, combinatorial analysis, Newton's binomial, probabilities, operations with complex numbers both in algebraic and trigonometric form), *advanced algebra* (permutations, operations with matrixes and determinants, determinants in analytical geometry, composition rules, algebraic structures, isomorphisms, classes of remainders, polynomials with complex and real coefficients, and theorems: Bezout, Horner, Viete), *geometry and trigonometry* (operations with vectors, Ceva's Theorem, Menelaus' Theorem, colinearity, perpendicularity, the trigonometric circle and functions, trigonometric identities and equations, trigonometric theorems and applications in triangles and analytical geometry), <u>calculus</u> (sequences and limits, limits of functions, continuity, derivatives, L'Hospital rule, asymptotes, application of first and second derivatives in the study and graphing of functions, primitives, integration formulas and the definite integral with applications in areas and volumes, integration by parts and by substitution, and integration of rational functions).

IG: Please describe the admittance to higher education procedure in Romania before and after 1989.

LD: I will refer only to the state (public) universities, since I am not familiar enough with private institutions of higher education. First, all applicants must have passed the Baccalaureate exam, and due to the in-depth high school curriculum in all subjects of study, students would choose a specialization as they apply to university. Before 1989, the entrance exam for specialization in mathematics, for example, consisted of three written tests in algebra, calculus, and geometry with trigonometry, while for engineering there were two written exams in mathematics and physics. This system was in place actually until 2000.

After 2000, admittance to higher education has been diversified. Some universities use one 4-hour written exam, while others use a criteria based on the students' grades in high school and predominantly the grade from the Baccalaureate exam.

IG: What options do high school graduates have with respect to higher education in Romania?

LD: Our graduates can opt for a variety of post-secondary education avenues. They can seek a 3-year Diploma de Licenta with specific specialization that can be followed by a 2-year Master's degree that requires a thesis, or they can follow a 2-year program of specialization for which they are not required Diploma de Baccalaureate except in the medical field.

IG: Please describe your classroom teaching activity, including home work, attendance, number of hours per week, class length, etc.

LD: Over a 9th through 12th grade program, the secondary education institution where I teach (industrial high school) offers professional qualifications in mechanics, chemistry, tourism, and public food service. We teach three hours of mathematics per week and they can be scheduled in either three or two different days. Secondary education institutions that don't provide trade qualification (theoretical high schools) teach four hours per week and in the 11th and 12th grades they teach five hours per week, and they can be scheduled at most two hours in the same day, with a ten-minute break. A regular class period consists of attendance check, brief homework check, explanations on last minute homework questions, review of concepts needed for the subsequent lecture, presentation of new concepts which is based on problems solved on the board with student participation, brief review of the new concepts, and homework assigning with occasional clarifications. There is a prescribed number of students per class, 28, but the actual number can be between 20 and 32. Recently, the Ministry of Education provides financing according to the number of students, so occasionally there can be salary problems for faculty and staff.

IG: What is the student evaluation system: grade scale, homework grades, tests, quizzes, finals?

LD: The grade scale is from 1 (lowest) to 10 (highest), and the minimum passing grade is 5. In general, students are evaluated in class on written pop-quizzes from the respective day's assignment and scheduled comprehensive tests over several lessons or a chapter. Homework is rarely graded. Some teachers grade students for work they are asked to do on the blackboard, but I don't, since I don't think this is an objective grading. Some teachers also use occasional take-home projects for grading, but in general the written testing is used because the final semester examination is a written comprehensive final. As far as the number of grades per semester is concerned, each student must have a number of grades equal to the number of hours per week in the respective subject of study. At the end of the semester we have a final examination that counts as 25% of the semester grade.

IG: How do you incorporate, if at all, technology in the process of teaching mathematics?

LD: We don't use pocket calculators or computers in the classroom; we encourage mental or written calculations because students are not allowed to use calculators on exams. We do have a computer lab but it is not used very much in the teaching of mathematics. There are software programs on different mathematical themes and students find them interesting and attractive. However, since class time is limited and loaded with rich curriculum, and since the Baccalaureate exam together with higher education entrance exams require work by hand, such programs are not used very much. My opinion is that they should not be used in the actual teaching, but they can be used as additional tools for practice or review.

IG: Do you use group or collaborative activities in the classroom? If you do, please describe them.

LD: I don't use group work in class due to the high volume of material we need to cover and to the large class size. I feel it is very difficult to implement successful group work which would lead to disorder and a playing atmosphere. On the other hand, I engage my students in the process of teaching and learning, encouraging them to suggest and justify their choices in solving different math problems as we work together.

IG: What is the implication of the Ministry of Education in pedagogical activities (design of different programs, teacher evaluation, etc.)?

LD: The Ministry of Education determines the number of hours for each course of study and establishes the curriculum along with common objectives to follow. They also determine how education cycles and final exams are organized, along with the curriculum required at these exams (national evaluation after 8th grade, and the Baccalaureate exam after 12th grade). The Ministry aproves a number of alternative textbooks for each course of study, from which teachers can select. The Ministry also oversees the organization of math competitions for students (the local, district, and national Olympiads, and other competitions). As secondary education teachers are required eventually to pass an examination in order to gain a definitive status, while senior teachers aspire to higher order in their profession, the Ministry of Education organizes and sets requirements for such examinations. The Ministry is represented by a special Educational Committee (EC) in each district of Romania, which oversees closely the entire educational activity in schools. The EC organizes informational meetings with teachers in each subject of study. The EC organizes regional professional development conferences, and organizes the hiring and the transfer of teachers in the district. Special EC members run occasional inspections in different schools, and these can be routine, requested, or triggered by possible educational problems (discipline, complaints, students' attendance or dropout, etc.). Such visits can also be conducted directly by the Ministry of Education. In addition, the EC is responsible for checking school documents (grades, attendance, sanctions, etc.), and is charged to reward certain teachers for excellence according to predetermined criteria. The EC should run the search and hiring process of school Directors, a process which unfortunately has been neglected recently. Instead, directors are politically nominated, which gravely undermines the education process.

IG: And, finally, what are the professional development requirements set by the Ministry of Education and how can teachers fulfil such requirements?

LD: Each district has in place an educational center responsible to organize professional activities, each counting as a number of credits. Each teacher has the obligation to complete 90 credits over every 5 years. Such activities are also organized by universities, and most of them are free. However, there are some professional development courses for which teachers must pay the registration fee, unless their institutions can cover it.

I would like to thank Mrs. Ligia Darau for her detailed answers in this email interview, and to wish her well in all walks of life.

12

Beautiful Mathematics in Nature

The deep emotional conviction of the presence of a superior reasoning power, which is revealed in the incomprehensible universe, forms my idea of God.

Albert Einstein

More often than not students affirm a dislike of mathematics, and this feeling is shared by many people in all walks of life. I find it a little odd since mathematical concepts, in one form or another, are used virtually everywhere, as we very well know. There must be an explanation for such a negative feeling about mathematics, and some of the reasons I can think of have to do with the teaching of this universally needed discipline. That is where the teacher and teacher's academic and pedagogical preparation come in. I say the teacher because it is true that, besides the required course work for a teaching degree, this noble profession does imply a special kind of personality and character, traits that can also be developed through consistent practice and devotion.

In this respect, it is never too late to remedy the situation if need be. With patience, skill, and personal determination, mathematics instructors can learn to present to students at any age the applicability and beauty of their subject, along with subtle interconnections between different areas of mathematics, and also between mathematics and other sciences such as physics, chemistry, biology, astronomy, and finance. Indeed, there is usefulness, connectivity, and beauty in mathematics, and each should be made visible if we are to reawaken the attractiveness of one of the most universal fields of modern education.

That is where mathematics in nature comes in as an optimal avenue to illustrate some of the natural beauty of this subject. Away from pure abstraction and dryness, nature offers some of the most attractive mathematical patterns and shapes for which one can hope. In the following I will just list a number of such examples while I encourage the reader to further explore this subject; libraries, book stores, and the internet are great sources of meaningful information.

Palm Tree in Portugal

The Golden Rectangle and Spirals

If one is asked to draw a rectangle at random, more often than not, she or he will not draw a heavily disproportionate rectangle. What I mean, for example, is that one will draw more or less an esthetic rectangle, a 'good looking' rectangle so that the length is not ten times longer than the width. From the time of the founders of geometry as we practice it today, the ancient Greeks 2500 years ago, esthetics were important. This is obvious as we admire architecture so craftily created back then. Regarding the rectangular shape, it has been established that one proportion in particular between the length and the width of a rectangle stood out esthetically.

And that is the so called *golden ratio*. Simply put, the golden ratio is 1.6108...., where the '....' means that the decimals never stop and never repeat. That makes this ratio an irrational number, which means that it cannot be written in a fraction form. A classical equation that leads to Phi, the golden ratio, is this:

$$\varphi = 1 + \frac{1}{\varphi}.$$

After solving, this equation renders the solution: $\varphi = \frac{1+\sqrt{5}}{2}$, which is the irrational number 1.6108.... In the meantime, Phi can also be expressed in a so called 'continued fraction' form like this:

$$\varphi = 1 + \cfrac{1}{1 + \cfrac{1}{1 + \cfrac{1}{1 + \cfrac{1}{1 + \cdots}}}},$$

where the further we push the calculations the closer we get to the irrational number 1.6108.... Yet, one other perspective of Phi is the following equation involving the length (l) and the width (w) of the *golden rectangle*:

$$\frac{l}{w} = \frac{w}{l} + 1.$$

If we solve this equation for l, we obtain the desired ratio: $l = \varphi w$, or $\varphi = \frac{l}{w}$.

To illustrate Phi in nature, let's start by watching closely the arrangement of the seeds of a sunflower. The plant cleverly grows its seeds in a spiral shape, and the purpose for this is to allow energy from the Sun to be received equally by all the seeds. As they are manifested by the mother plant, seeds don't grow in a linear shape which is generated by finite fractions, since a linear pattern would force some seeds to be obscured by others. So, each subsequent seed anchors itself at a turn from the linear direction generated by the previous two. Now get ready for this: the turn is exactly 0.6108.... which is the decimal part of Phi (a 1 for the integer part simply means a complete circle). Therefore, within the universal intelligence that encompasses our world, the sunflower plant has learned somehow to manifest the most efficient pattern for the distribution of its seeds.

As probably expected, this same pattern of a spiral created based on the golden ratio, is widely spread in nature. In this respect, leaves of plants and petals of flowers arrange themselves in spirals also. Of course, the reason is the same: nature strives to optimize the use of available energy by implementation of precise mathematical patterns to distribute it evenly and, as we can appeal to natural intelligence, fairly to its precious community members.

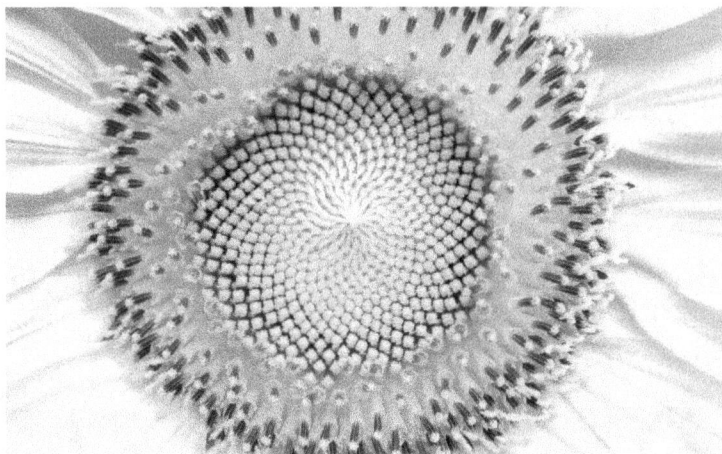

Sunflower Seeds

Let us now look farther out, much farther out. Yes, you guessed it: the Milky Way, our galaxy, from its conception arranged its billions of stars in the beautiful pattern of a spinning spiral. Why? Can we invoke the model of an intelligent sunflower seed arrangement to depict the extraordinary intelligence involved in the galactic spiral pattern? I think we can. We can even speculate that, as the sunflower learned (or it was taught!) the ideal pattern for its seeds to equally share the energy of the Sun, Milky Way learned how to optimally distribute its stars and their planets away from the black hole at its center for their protection and for them to absorb proportionally the energy of the universe, as our solar system implicitly does. With this last vision before us, can we say that in fact patterns on Earth are but miniatures of much larger and more powerful mathematical laws that govern the universe? They certainly appear that way. And here is a further thought: are they interconnected? In light of the latest advances in quantum mechanics relative to the universal connection, which closely parallels Eastern philosophy, it seems very logical to see Earth and everything on it in perfect alignment with the universe. And yes, the beauty of mathematical patterns can set us on a revelatory path to the understanding of life on Earth and our place as human beings in the larger scheme of things: it's all in an intriguing order since WE ARE ALL ONE.

Image of the Milky Way

Fibonacci Patterns

The famous Fibonacci sequence of natural numbers follows this simple rule: each number is the sum of the two numbers before it. So, if we start with 1, we obtain: 1, 2, 3, 5, 8, 13, 21, 34, 55, 89, 144, 233, 377, and so on. Not only are Fibonacci numbers used in mathematics as an example in the study of sequences and series, but they are also connected to nature. Most flowers grow petals in numbers that closely follow this sequence. In other words, there are very few flowers that have 4, 6, or 7 petals. In fact the 4-petal leaf of clover, for example, is considered an anomaly.

And another pattern arises from the Fibonacci sequence, one that is tightly connected to the golden ratio. As we calculate the ratio of every pair of consecutive numbers, we notice that, moving through the sequence, the decimal values navigate around the irrational number Phi, 1.6108.... And here are some examples:

$$\frac{3}{2} = 1.5, \frac{5}{3} = 1.666...., \frac{8}{5} = 1.6, \frac{13}{8} = 1.625, \frac{21}{13} = 1.615384615,$$

$$\frac{34}{21} = 1.619047619, \frac{55}{34} = 1.617647059, \frac{89}{55} = 1.6181818...$$

$$\frac{144}{89} = 1.617977529, \frac{233}{144} = 1.618055556,$$

$$\frac{377}{233} = 1.618025751.$$

Since we have already seen that the golden ratio Phi is instrumental in generating spirals, this pattern should lead us to think of a connection between the Fibonacci sequence and the spiral shape. And they do connect. Take the pineapple scales' arrangement and the pinecone's degenerated leaves distribution. There are several spirals in each and they follow ratios close to Phi based on Fibonacci pattern inherent in their numbers.

So, although we cannot say that there is an immutable natural law that governs rigidly through strict mathematical models, we can definitely say that nature strongly tends to follow stable and ideal patterns. Perhaps such near misses off rigidity allows for flexibility and creativity in the natural realm. In turn, we should be grateful for the impressive variety of life forms that embrace us on our wonderful planet Earth, and mathematical modeling is here to testify to the natural order that appears intelligent obviously present in the entire web of interconnections.

Hexagons

As we have already seen, geometry is not only a fascinating branch of mathematics but it has direct and very interesting applications in nature. Yes, humans heavily use geometry in construction and engineering, but it is evident that the natural world implements regular geometrical shapes as a way to optimize its existence. In this respect, the perfect symmetry of a regular hexagon is naturally crafted into the beautiful shape of a snowflake, for instance.

Hexagonal Honeycomb

To consider another example, take the honeybees. It is not at random that bees build their honeycombs in the shape of regular hexagons. A regular hexagon has six equal sides and, consequently, each of its angles measures exactly 120°. This is an important fact since it allows three adjacent hexagons of the same size to fit perfectly together at any of their vertices (there is no space lost between them because they complete a full circle: 3 times 120° is 360°). As far as bee ingenuity is concerned, a given surface area can be covered with the maximum number of hexagonal cells that require a minimum amount of wax. Moreover, since the queen bee lays an egg in every cell, the access to a hexagonal cell is much easier than to a square cell, for example. Compared to the more open 120° angles of a hexagon, the 90° angles of a square are not optimal in terms of bees' activity of depositing or extracting honey. In fact, beside squares, hexagons are the regular polygons with the largest angles that fit perfectly at every vertex while providing an almost circular 'entrance' to the cell. In the meantime, the circular shape itself is also not optimal since there will be lost space between such cells along with an excess of wax needed to build them. So the question is: how did the honey bees 'engineer' this marvel? Who or what instructed them to select this exact shape for their honey combs? One could argue that 'natural selection' was at work from time immemorial, but to select 'naturally' still implies a purposeful intent for the optimal choice between, let's say, a square and a hexagonal shape. They, and get ready for this, had to realize, even if it took millions of years, that one shape is more economical than another. But realizing underlines some level of thinking, hence intelligence and/or order. Moreover, once discovered (or implanted in their DNA), the hexagonal shape has, to present knowledge, never been abandoned or altered. Therefore, we identify here yet another clear example of how the universal intelligent order that permeates all things works, including the use of mathematical models. Consequently, since we are analyzing this consciously, we are a way for the universe to know itself, as the late physicist Carl Sagan stated.

With these examples in mind, we can conclude that in our search for beauty in the world we are gently assisted by nature itself as it is implementing clear mathematical concepts. Accidentally? I don't think so. As we feel what beauty really means, we can see that nature likes beauty as well. Not only that, but nature is amazingly on purpose in selecting those mathematical patterns that are effective and economical. The beauty of the shape of a spiral is evident as we admire the Milky Way or a sunflower. Flowers, more often than not, grow their petals following closely the Fibonacci numbers. Bees, generation after generation, create regular hexagonal well-built honeycombs. So, next time we look at an image of our galaxy, next time we smell a beautiful daisy, or next time we taste sweet honey, they will all speak to us in a different language. This is the language of innate beauty often manifested within mathematical intelligent and orderly patterns. We should grow to understand and appreciate them most importantly because we are all sharing the same beautiful natural environment. Moreover, since our biological planetary habitat is actually a closed in system, we can definitely say that, living an interdependent life, we are all interconnected, which should awaken a great sense of union and responsibility in all of us as I demonstrated in my earlier book WE ARE ALL ONE.

13

Find the Best Solution

Choose always the way that seems the best, however rough it may be; custom will soon render it easy and agreeable.

Pythagoras

I love simple. Really! And I think we all do. After all, who likes complicated? In this respect, what better educational area than mathematics do we have to seek simple? The solving of many math problems lends itself to a variety of approaches, some simpler than others. As students, but more importantly teachers, we should all be searching for the best, the simplest solution we can find to any proposed problem. Mastering of mathematics is best displayed by unveiling the simplest and the most elegant solution the more complicated the problem is. Benefits are many and they are monumental. In most cases, the simplest solution implies the shortest or the fastest, which automatically saves us time. One can imagine how important this is on timed tests and exams, and, for example, placement tests, expanding to SAT and GRE exams. Not only is this a time and therefore, money saver, but it is also a tremendous confidence builder. Indeed, being able to solve problems multiple ways, offers choices that can boost self-confidence, which can implicitly lead to higher success rates in all walks of life.

One ancient classical example of a mathematical theorem comes to mind: the Pythagorean Theorem. There are literally hundreds and hundreds of proofs accumulated over centuries of research by mathematicians and other people of science. In my volume entitled *Teach For Life* I treated the famous theorem in detail, illustrating some very simple but interesting proves, even one offered by a former U.S. president.

In this volume I will include a few more examples of what I consider better approaches to solving problems from fundamental algebra.

Example 1.

This is a simple equation given in proportion form: $\frac{3x}{5} = \frac{18}{25}$.

In order to solve it, one could employ a standard strategy that recalls a basic property of proportions: the cross products are equal. Therefore: $(3x) \cdot 25 = 5 \cdot 18$, or $75x = 90$. In the end we solve for x by dividing both sides of the equation by 75, so we have: $x = \frac{90}{75}$, which after simplifications leads to the final solution: $x = \frac{6}{5}$.

A second approach could be to multiply both sides of the original equation by the reciprocal of $\frac{3}{5}$ in order to isolate x on the left side: $\frac{5}{3} \cdot \frac{3x}{5} = \frac{5}{3} \cdot \frac{18}{25}$. After simplifications we obtain: $x = \frac{6}{5}$.

A third strategy could reach the same result by the "common denominator" approach. If a proportion has the same denominator on both sides of the equal sign, the denominators can be dropped. In order to reach this goal all we have to do is multiply the numerator and denominator of the fraction on the left by 5. As we drop the denominators, this leads to: $15x = 18$, and, after we divide both sides by 15 and simplify, we find the solution $x = \frac{6}{5}$.

Yet, what I consider the nicest, simplest, and most elegant approach, uses another general property of equations: we can divide *all* the numerators or denominators by their greatest common factor. Consequently, a close examination of the original equation, $\frac{3x}{5} = \frac{18}{25}$, offers the simplest approach: dividing the numerators by 3 and the denominators by 5, we reach our solution most quickly: $x = \frac{6}{5}$.

Example 2.

The second example I would like to consider has to do with simplifying complex fractions. Let's assume we want to simplify this expression:

$$\frac{(5a^{-2} - 5b^{-2})}{(a^{-1} - b^{-1})}.$$

The traditional procedure is to first convert negative exponents to positive, and done properly, we obtain:

$$\frac{\left(\frac{5}{a^2} - \frac{5}{b^2}\right)}{\left(\frac{1}{a} - \frac{1}{b}\right)}.$$

As we find common denominators for each of the numerator and the denominator of the complex fraction, we have:

$$\frac{\frac{(5b^2 - 5a^2)}{(a^2 b^2)}}{\frac{b-a}{ab}}.$$

After factoring the numerator completely (which implies a difference of squares) and multiplying by the reciprocal of the fraction from the denominator, the expression becomes:

$$\frac{5(b-a)(b+a)}{(a^2 b^2)} \cdot \frac{ab}{b-a}.$$

By simplifying the common factors from the numerators and denominators, we arrive at the final answer:

$$\frac{5(b+a)}{ab}.$$

However, here is a simpler and more elegant approach a student of mine tried, although he was only partially successful. After we factor 5 as a common factor, we can factor the rest of the numerator as a difference of squares with negative exponents, so the expression becomes:

$$\frac{[5(a^{-1} - b^{-1})(a^{-1} + b^{-1})]}{(a^{-1} - b^{-1})}.$$

After the obvious simplification, we obtain:

$$5(a^{-1} + b^{-1}).$$

Since final answers should not contain negative exponents, now we convert negative exponents to positive and we have:

$$5(\frac{1}{a} + \frac{1}{b}).$$

By simply finding the common denominator in the parenthesis and making the proper adjustments, we get the final answer:

$$\frac{5(b+a)}{ab}.$$

Example 3.

As we already saw in the previous example, factoring is a very important concept in mathematics. Not only is it used to simplify algebraic expressions, but it is also useful in solving equations that help solve application problems and also graphing functions. Therefore, I will consider the case of factoring a trinomial, which is among the most disputed factoring strategies. The trinomial I choose to factor is:

$$6x^2 - 29x + 28.$$

There are several methods of factoring a trinomial: 1) we can use the quadratic formula to find the solutions of the associated quadratic equation and then rebuild the linear factors, 2) we can use the so called "master product rule" (also called the "grouping method"), or 3) we can employ what I consider the easier, simpler, and faster method: the trial and error that I call 'the 'ANTI-FOIL' method that consists of reversing FOIL (the procedure of multiplying two binomials: First, Outer, Inner, Last). The first approach is pretty self-explanatory, so I will treat the second and third by evidencing their main characteristics.

The "grouping method" entails two steps that are rarely explained to students. In other words, it prescribes what to do but not why we do it; this in itself should be a no-no in mathematical logic since we should make a special effort on understanding *why* and not just *what* and *how* in the solving of a problem. The first step states: multiply the first and the last coefficients of the trinomial, and in this case we obtain 168. As it is generally proposed to students, the teaching fails to explain why we do this, which is the main problem I have with it (of course it can be proven, but that leads to a pretty abstract procedure). The second step requires us to find (keep in mind!) two factors of 168 whose sum is 29! Is that an easy thing to do? I don't think so; in most cases it is not, and it leads, nevertheless, to trial and error. Again, the second step is also not explained to the students. In the end, though, the method works by writing the trinomial as a four-term polynomial that will eventually be factored by the grouping method like this:

$$6x^2 - 21x - 8x + 28 = 3x(2x - 7) - 4(2x - 7) =$$
$$(2x - 7)(3x - 4).$$

The third method I propose as the simplest and most logical to me is based on reversing FOIL (the ANTI-FOIL, as I call it), which already gives a clear answer to the crucial question: WHY? The initial step is to factor the first term as 2x and 3x, and setting the two binomials like this:

$$(2x \quad m)(3x \quad n).$$

Then, and this is when it gets most interesting, we need to find (keep in mind) two factors of 28, m and n, to complete the binomials such that when we add the Outer (2xn) and Inner (3xm) products, to obtain 29x; this is completely logical since it is part of FOIL. As we can see, by using our number sense, we have to select from three pairs of factors of 28 (2 and 14, 4 and 7, and 1 and 28). Of course, combining these with the chosen coefficients 2 and 3, we are facing six alternatives. Now here is my unique contribution to simplifying this process significantly: we cannot consider using an even number for m, because then we could take out 2 as a common factor from that binomial which was not possible from the beginning, so it is wrong. This way we limit our options to basically one: use 7 for m and 4 for

n. This turns out to be the right combination and the problem is solved as soon as we adjust the signs, which I suggest should be done at the end of the procedure:

$$(2x - 7)(3x - 4).$$

One could see, therefore, that since in this method we are reversing the well-understood FOIL, the steps make sense even if at times we might need to try a couple of combinations to reach the correct one. The benefit versus the 'grouping method' is that this is logical and the numbers with which we work are much smaller – recount that then we had to find two factors of 168 whose sum is 29: not an easy thing to do, in addition to being unexplained.

Example 4.

Now I would like to offer an example from the field of systems of equations as we use them to solve application problems. Two classical approaches to solving linear systems of equations with two or more variables are: by substitution or elimination. The idea is to arrive at an equation with only one variable that we can easily solve. However, in some cases either method will lead to more complicated work than we prefer. Many such situations lend themselves to much better although non-orthodox approaches. Here is a clear example of the use of systems of linear equations to solve an application problem:

"Multiples of two numbers x and y are used in two different ways to create two sets of supplementary angles. If the first pair of angles is 21x and 12y and the second is 19x and 13y, find x and y."

Based on the definition of supplementary angles we create the system of two equations with two variables:

$$21x + 12y = 180$$
$$19x + 13y = 180$$

Even with limited experience with respect to solving systems of equations we notice that substitution or elimination will not work very well or as rapidly as we would like. That is why I propose an alternative approach: first, subtract the two equations side by side. We obtain:

$$2x - y = 0.$$

From this much simpler equation we can derive a substitute for y, which is:

$$y = 2x.$$

Now we substitute y by 2x in the first equation and we have:

$$21x + 12(2x) = 180.$$

This is a linear equation with only one variable, which we can quickly solve:

$$21x + 24x = 180$$
$$45x = 180$$
$$x = \frac{180}{45}$$
$$x = 4$$

As soon as we have the value of x, all we need to do to find y is to substitute x by 4 into $y = 2x$. Therefore, $y = 2 \cdot 4$, so $y = 8$.

Example 5.

Another example is from quadratic equations, an area with vast applications in all of mathematics. Here are some classical questions: "If 3 and 5 are the solutions of a quadratic equation, find such an equation." Or, "If 3 and 5 are the x-intercepts of a quadratic function, find such a function." Or, "If 3 and 5 are two of the zeros of a given third degree real polynomial function, what is the third zero?"

In this respect, the standard procedure to find the quadratic trinomial with the given zeros is to build the two linear binomials from which the zeros can be derived, and multiplying them, usually by FOIL, we have:

$$(x - 3)(x - 5) = x^2 - 5x - 3x + 15.$$

Thus we obtain: $x^2 - 8x + 15$.

However, if we remember a less used but easy to prove relationship which states briefly that the sum (s) of the solutions of a quadratic equation $(ax^2 + bx + c = 0)$ is $s = -\frac{b}{a}$ and their product (p) is $p = \frac{c}{a}$ (dividing $ax^2 + bx + c = 0$ by 'a' leads to: $x^2 + \frac{b}{a}x + \frac{c}{a} = 0$), the equation can be rebuilt easily this way:

$$x^2 - sx + p = 0.$$

In this respect, the problem becomes very simple since $s = 3 + 5 = 8$, $p = 3 \cdot 5 = 15$, so the equation becomes:

$$x^2 - 8x + 15 = 0.$$

This approach is even more beneficial when we deal with complex solutions. To illustrate this, let's assume the solutions are $3 + 2i$ and $3 - 2i$. If we are to follow the standard procedure to find the respective quadratic equation, we are supposed to multiply $[x - (3 + 2i)][x - (3 - 2i)]$, which leads to:

$$(x - 3 - 2i)(x - 3 + 2i).$$

As opposed to multiplying by the long procedure (distributing every term from the first parenthesis over the second), the easiest way to multiply *these* two tri-nomials is to recognize that in fact we are dealing with a difference of squares:

$$(x - 3)^2 - (2i)^2.$$

Therefore, we have: $x^2 - 6x + 9 - 4i^2$.

Remembering that $i^2 = -1$, we obtain the final answer:

$$x^2 - 6x + 9 - 4(-1) = x^2 - 6x + 9 + 4 = x^2 - 6x + 13.$$

However, if we use the sum and product of the solutions to build the quadratic equation (described before), we quickly find:

$$s = (3 + 2i) + (3 - 2i) = 6, \text{ and}$$
$$p = (3 + 2i)(3 - 2i) = 9 - 4i^2 = 9 - 4(-1) = 9 + 4 = 13.$$

Consequently, based on $x^2 - sx + p = 0$, the equation we are seeking can be found much easier this way:

$$x^2 - 6x + 13 = 0.$$

Example 6.

I will close with an example from polynomials, more specifically concerning powers of binomials, which have a multitude of applications including calculations of probabilities. In this respect, let's consider the binomial $(a + b)$ whose coefficients (the numbers in front of the variables) are 1 and 1. The coefficients of $(a + b)^2$ are 1, 2, and 1, and they can be obtained by multiplying as follows:

$$(a + b)(a + b) = a^2 + ab + ba + b^2 = a^2 + 2ab + b^2.$$

Then we can obtain the coefficients of $(a + b)^3$ by multiplying $(a + b)$ three times, or by multiplying the previous power $(a^2 + 2ab + b^2)$ by another $(a + b)$, and we arrive at: $a^3 + 3a^2b + 3ab^2 + b^3$; so the coefficients are: 1, 3, 3, and 1. Worth noticing already is that in our answers, so far, the variables are following a well-determined pattern: the exponents of 'a' are decreasing consecutively, as those of 'b' are increasing. But, as we can see, this work becomes very tedious due to the process of polynomial multiplication. That is why for higher exponents we use better methods. One of them involves use of combinations to find the respective coefficients, which after a while become also too cumbersome to calculate, so I will not describe this method here.

However, my favorite is Pascal's triangle, and here it is:

```
                      1
                    1   1
                  1   2   1
                1   3   3   1
              1   4   6   4   1
            1   5  10  10   5   1
          1   6  15  20  15   6   1
        1   7  21  35  35  21   7   1
      1   8  28  56  70  56  28   8   1
    1   9  36  84 126 126  84  36   9   1
  1  10  45 120 210 252 210 120  45  10   1
```

I encourage the reader to take a few moments to examine the triangle and identify all visible patterns including the symmetry about an imaginary vertical line through the middle. It is obvious that the first three lines of this table are the coefficients of the first three powers of (a + b), so the logical conclusion emerges: every successive line contains the coefficients of the following power of this binomial.

The triangle might look complex at first, but one simple way to build it is to notice that every number starting with line two down, is the sum of the two numbers above it. Consequently, based on all the previous considerations, if we need to find the expansion of, for example $(a + b)^7$, all we have to do is to use as coefficients the numbers on the 7th line in the triangle, and to arrange the exponents of the variables as mentioned above. The polynomial is easy to write:

$(a + b)^7 = a^7 + 7a^6b + 21a^5b^2 + 35a^4b^3 + 35a^3b^4 + 21a^2b^5 + 7ab^6 + b^7$.

I hope these examples are sufficiently illustrative of the beneficial search for better solutions in mathematics. Not only does this save time, improve our versatility, and increase self-confidence, but also shows the beauty and flexibility inherent in mathematical explorations. After all, I consider the pursuit of better solutions in all subjects of study as one of the main reasons for general education.

14

Cherish Freedom

The best road to progress is freedom's road.
John F. Kennedy

The world displays an impressive range of levels of personal and national freedom: from the freedom as we know it in the West, to the dictatorships of modern day Middle East and Africa, and to the brutal communist regimes still in place in Cuba, North Korea, and China. If we navigate back in time about a quarter of a century, we land on a period that changed history in Eastern Europe. "Mr. Gorbachev, tear down this wall!" marked the beginning of the collapse of communism in U.S.S.R. and the many countries that had been so enslaved the moment WWII ended. Of course, the liberation process was much more complex than a simple result of a deeply felt "request" verbalized so eloquently by President Reagan in West Berlin, then in West Germany. Indeed, the many significant cultural, social, and national differences between the countries behind the Iron Curtain made the 1989 anti-communist revolutions unique in every one of them.

Elsewhere, the U.S.A. and the rest of the world were patiently watching as millions upon millions of people were gaining back their freedom from the oppressive ideological systems that persisted for almost half a century in Eastern Europe, and since 1917 in Russia. These governments preached democracy, but in reality practiced brutal dictatorship, which was the only way they were able to hold on to the power they stole almost overnight. At last, all populations of the Eastern Bloc became once again free to craft their own future in true democracies.

But how was it possible for so many countries that were free before WWII to suddenly become enslaved by a political system not of their choice? The birth of such a system was in 1917 when the Russian Communist Revolution took place. It is significant to know that prior to 1917 the Russian people had not known capitalism; the industrial revolution of the West had not reached them. In the United States of America, Henry Ford, for example, improved the assembly line, raised wages for his employees, instituted 8-hour workdays in 5-day workweeks and made cars affordable to the middle class. At the same time, the Russians were still living under the tsarist agricultural feudal regime. Within such realities the young communist party surrounding Lenin, crudely killed Tsar Nicholas II and his entire Romanov family, as they plunged the enormous country of Russia into a brand new system, communism, which up to that time had only been a fantasy in the books of Marx and Engels.

So it was actualized in Russia, and, with the Allies' victory in WWII, paired with some debatable and irrational international treaties thrown together behind closed doors, the Eastern part of Europe fell under Russian communist domination. That is exactly how the communist destiny of my native country, Romania, was imposed and sealed in 1945. As direct neighbors of the U.S.S.R., behind the newly created borders in detriment of the very nation of Romania, the Romanians were taken hostage basically overnight by a small and naïve young communist party, substantially helped by the cruel Stalinist regime next door.

But it wasn't to be that easy; not all Romanians gave in without any opposition. The decade or so following WWII is known as the bloodiest in terms of merciless retaliation draconically practiced by the Romanian Secret Police (the Securitate), which was ordered to torment and punish any form of insubordination. In this respect, well-documented research conducted after the 1989 anticommunist revolution in Romania, unearthed several mass graves. From the late 1940s and well into the 1950s, the Securitate dumped into these mass graves young dead bodies of the freedom fighters the Securitate cowardly executed. During those years, students, educators, and others aligned themselves with older and already established anticommunist organizations in efforts to preserve the educational, economical, and political freedoms Romanians had created, nurtured, and enjoyed for decades prior to the U.S.S.R. backed takeover of their country.

One such young mind was Ioan Glajar, my father. In 1948, at 19 years of age in his final academic year of what today is high school, he decided to join a youth anticommunist organization in Fagaras, district of Brasov, but in a non-combative roll, as he later declared. As fate had it, one evening, at the end of a meeting with some of the members of his group, he decided to go home instead of joining the others in the mountains as they were planning further action. The very next morning Securitate officers showed up at my grandparents' house searching for him. In the tension of the situation, my father managed to slip to his grandmother who was nearby, a piece of paper he had in his pocket. That piece of paper contained and listed the names of the other members of the group. Understanding the gravity of the entire scenario, she found the opportune moment and swallowed the small paper in one take. However, not incriminating the others did not save my father: he was arrested, judged, convicted, and sentenced to one year of prison for conspiring against the well-being of the newly created 'democracy' under the communist regime of Romania. Meanwhile, several of the members who escaped in the mountains had been killed as they opposed arrest.

My grandparents were devastated as they were watching my father's future shattered in front of their eyes. They had sacrificed all they had to keep him in school, which was not easy those days, and now his chance to become a mathematics or physics professor, subjects he liked and excelled at, was completely lost. After the one year of imprisonment, although he managed to finish high school and was ready for the college entrance exams, my father was not accepted by any university in the country: he was on the black list of anti-communism fighters.

What was there to do? He loved books and he wanted to study especially since he did not intend to follow his parents' way of life as keepers of their small farm. The only escape that shined at the end of the tunnel of academic impossibilities he faced was the study of theology, which meant in fact that he would become a priest in the Christian Orthodox denomination that was tolerated by the new political party as a clever strategy to prevent mass rebellion. In spite of the communist repulsion towards religion, admission to theological seminary was not guarded as closely as admission to regular state universities that were under the Ministry of Education (Karl Marx on religion: "Religion is the opium of the people").

So, then started a series of meaningful ironies that shaped the rest of my father's life and implicitly the lives of all of us members of the family. First, as I mentioned, he did not intend to study theology, but due to his political choice in a communist country, theology was his only chance to follow his academic calling. Therefore he completed the required four years of theological studies. Second, after his graduation from the theological seminary, and after he even studied three years for a magister (master) in theology degree, he did not want to become a priest, hoping to secure a position as a librarian. But, since none were open at that time, and since he was in dire need of a job to support his family, my father had to accept the first available employment as a priest. And the third irony was that, although he never wanted to become a priest in his home village, the only position for a priest that suddenly opened up happened to be exactly in his own village, so he had to take it. The year was 1959 when the Securitate started a long-term drama on our entire family.

My Father's Secret Police File

We have seen, so far, how hard the Romanian Secret Police fought to establish the dictatorial authority of the new regime in a previously free country. It is also worth enumerating some of the freedoms the Romanian population had lost to communism. In this respect, the country became a huge prison for all, except, of course, for some elected members of the Communist Party. Close to 20 million people were virtually imprisoned. It was all but impossible to travel abroad, especially to the West. Open international cultural exchanges had been drastically limited and those with non-communist countries were eliminated almost completely. Under the precepts of socialism and egalitarianism even highly qualified professionals such as doctors, teachers, and engineers were paid little and about the same. Consequently a system of illegitimate income creation and bribes found its way into a society struggling to survive. Freedom of the press and freedom of speech were radically eroded to a level where every honest Romanian not in tandem with the communist party was afraid to utter any words in disaccord with the official propaganda. Censorship on all fronts had expanded and a sophisticated net of spies and informers was put in place as the regime offered personal rewards to those who would agree to inform the Securitate about subjects of interest. And the list of oppressions can be continued.

This is where my father's life serves as powerful testimony to the atrocities that the Romanian communist regime inflicted on the population. Out of fear of losing their grip on power, the Securitate instituted a complex top-secret system of information in order to collect, record, and store depositions from its informers ('sources') on selective people of interest ('objectives'). My father became such an 'objective.' Over the

40 years of this meticulous activity, thousands of files on 'objectives' were stored away by the Securitate all over the country. As an immediate outcome of incriminating files, many 'objectives' have met tragic destinies. Others, whose 'sources' were not able to collect direct evidence of anticommunist intent, were granted some lighter status, eventually being dropped from the list of 'objectives.'

After the 1989 successful anticommunist Revolution, most of the available files have been declassified and made available to researchers and 'objectives' or their families. That is how in 2014, since my father passed away in 2012, I secured a digital copy of his file. As I read the many reports (depositions made by the informers), George Orwell's "1984", the novel, came vividly to mind: Big Brother was alive and well in Romania during all those years but I didn't realize it until 1975 when my father secretly pointed it out to me as a life-saving warning. It happened on a park bench in Cluj a few days before my first semester as a student in higher education.

Immediately after he started his career as an Orthodox priest, due to his past as a member of an anticommunist organization, the Securitate placed my father under close observation. In a sustained effort to make him into an informer, they asked him to write by hand his autobiography, where, of course he was supposed to mention his one-year imprisonment, which he did. However, in spite of their efforts to blackmail him based on his past, he vehemently declined the 'invitation' to become a 'source' for the Securitate. Instead, he played the politically correct game by declaring that out of his love for his country he will do what he could to assist its progress as a democracy and he will always promote peace.

According to the files, the years that followed were marked by a well-organized informers' covert activity, and it is shocking to me today to be able to recognize some of them within the group of close friends, colleagues, or even neighbors of my father. Among several informers charged to observe him, one 'source' who was also a priest shocked me the most. He was reporting on my father's professional initiatives during regular meetings, the sermons he gave, the content of his talks, and how he was approaching his parishioners at a personal level. However, there was nothing incriminating. Another 'source' took advantage of his close friendship with my father and reported after every dinner or get together they had; again, with nothing incriminating. And a 'good' neighbor of ours, used every opportunity to report in detail even when my father was waiting for the bus, or, more importantly, when he was receiving guests: who they were, how long they stayed, and if they came by car, on motorcycle, or on foot. And yes, you guessed it: with nothing incriminating.

But the 'sources' did not limit their depositions just to my father's life. They had been instructed by their superiors (which is also documented in the files) to investigate the entire family. My mother, my grandparents and even us, the children (me and my sister) were not left out; apparently the Securitate wanted to make sure that my father did not conduct a double life by nurturing anticommunist ideas within the intimacy of his own household. However, the 'sources' have been clearly educated not to push the subject of discussion too hard toward politics or the state of affairs in the country. They were supposed to wait for the 'objective' (my father) to initiate such themes that could have possibly revealed his anticommunist side.

But it never surfaced; at least not in front of the 'sources.' From later discussions with my father on such subjects, it was clear to me that his detention at 19 years of age was powerful enough to prepare him to face the new regime in such a way that will prevent

Irie's Parents in 2009

future repercussions. Indeed, he was determined not to give anything away in public, and this was exactly due to the permanent fear of handing precious fuel to possible 'sources.' And he was right to suspect virtually anybody and everybody to be a 'source.' In fact, halfway jokingly, in the communist era we used to say that whenever two Romanians talk to each other in the street, one of them is an informer; so deep the lack of trust was, lack of freedom of expression, and the fear of cruel punishment.

In the end, the thousands of files documenting the cruelty with which the communist regime of Romania exercised its dictatorial oppression should constitute a great source of inspiration for future generations all around the globe as far as treasuring freedom is concerned. In this respect, a great number of these files are undisputable testimonies to much worse outcomes at the hands of the Securitate than what my father endured: 'objectives' lost jobs, were sentenced to long term prison terms, and many have simply disappeared as they were systematically killed. Obviously the communists' determination to stay in power was very resolved and extremely costly in both human lives destroyed and valuable resources wasted. In fact, the implementation, the expansion, and the preservation of communist ideology around the world (denial of freedom and basic human rights) are directly responsible for far more deaths than both World Wars combined.

Present times offer us more themes for reflection on human rights and freedom. Any intrusion into one's private life, facilitated by high-tech means, for example, is an affront to that person's individual freedom. Among the most remarkable traits of life in the changing world of the 21st century, freedom should be held high. From freedom of expression and access to education, to all other liberties preserved in the West, we should treasure and promote freedom on all continents; people all over the world should cherish freedom and responsibly aspire to it in all walks of life. As long as our endeavors are not self-destructive and are not practiced at the expense of other human beings or the environment, freedom should reign. People should be free to decide their immediate future and to craft their own destinies. In this respect, we should double our efforts to eliminate gender, religious, physical appearance, and racial discrimination as we should take to heart the lessons from the past. The dictatorships behind the Iron Curtain of the last century should serve as clear examples of unacceptable governing ideology. Consequently, the modern world should nurture all efforts for peace and freedom toward the abolition of any still remaining totalitarian regimes, as we strive to ensure a brighter future for the human race.

15

Decline of Mathematics Education in the U.S.

He who has a _why_ to live for can bear almost any _how_.
Friedrich Nietzsche

Modern days display an evident effort to water down the teaching of mathematics at all undergraduate levels. In fact, this movement was started decades ego and such teaching methodology has been described suggestively by friend and foe as new math, fuzzy math, everyday mathematics, consortium calculus, group-collaborative learning, modeling, and math emporiums where most of the 'teaching' is furnished by software programs. All these, and more, have been characterized as intrinsic components of a so-called 'socio-constructivist' approach to math education. Out goes the rigorous teaching based on strong number sense, memorization of formulas, and a clear logical understanding of mathematical concepts along with their interconnection based on skilled practice and use of dependable tools and procedures. Instead, comes a diluted 'conceptual' learning seemingly pretending that knowing something about math concepts is equivalent to proficiency in mathematics.

Even worse, and sadly so, there are some mathematics instructors and/or supervisors who actually promote a mechanical learning of mathematics under the precept that 'our students don't become math teachers, so they don't have to understand what they are doing.' And, to promote new non-pedagogical approaches, the affront to the true teaching of mathematics goes further when they use demeaning slogans such as: 'It is not your granddaddy's mathematics' or 'How to conquer the math monster' which amplifies the fear of mathematics that already exists in our society.

An alternative title to this essay can be, then, "Just Teach!" but a working title I had in mind was "The Illusion of Teaching Mathematics." In light of the developments in mathematics education described above, it is indeed an illusion of teaching mathematics. Therefore, I think it is worth observing a little closer any and all group-collaborative work in the classroom, mediated learning, the emporium model, online teaching, and online testing and/or grading, as all attempt to shape and diminish math education in the U.S. Such approaches clearly illustrate a departure from proven traditional teaching, hence "the illusion" of teaching mathematics. In fact, they are meant to replace the established lecture style with a 'feel-good' and don't-worry-about-real-learning approach by setting students in groups to basically teach each other, or by computers, where students are being taught mathematics by dry and insensitive pre-programmed software; both methods teach at best the "How?" but have little to do with really understanding mathematics: the

"Why?" In contrast, the traditional approach incorporates instructor's live presentation of new concepts, which is followed by examples that engage the students in the process of thinking logically about what they learn. The indispensable "Why?" in the teaching of mathematics is therefore answered on the spot in the classroom under the clear light of instructor's experience and expertise that spring from years of pedagogical experience, exploration and practice.

Of course, in the latter approach, the way an instructor structures the classroom activity varies from person to person, which makes it much more interesting and also worth investigating; after all, this is the best way to address the well-known reality of multiple intelligences that our students display so well. As an example, I would like to include here "How I Taught the Course" description of how I approach my class lecture, which is included in my required faculty evaluations package at my place of work.

"My general classroom activity is composed of four main sections:

1) Homework check period,
2) Homework quiz,
3) Instruction on the new section(s), and
4) Assigning daily homework with specific comments and examples.

Details:

1. During the first part of the class meeting, I cover all or most of the questions students might have from their homework. This also offers me a timely chance to identify students' problems and to re-explain some of the

contents of the previous material. Therefore, students are presented with explanations of the same concepts twice, and students who were absent from the previous class period can easily catch up.

2. Occasionally I give a quiz from the homework (very similar but not identical to the homework problems). A quiz consists of 3 to 5 exercises, and it takes about 10 to 15 minutes.

3. Then I start the new material. First, I describe the larger picture of the new concepts. I explain how they are connecting with the previous section(s) or chapter(s), and I present reasons for studying them (the need for the concepts in future math courses, applicability in "real" life, etc.). Second, I introduce new formulas, new general math concepts, with occasional proofs. Third, gradually throughout the lesson, I cover as many examples as possible (usually from the respective sections in the textbook) in order to illustrate the new material. Very often I also offer what I consider better alternatives to the procedures already presented, so that students can select the methods with which they feel more comfortable. My major concern is for students to understand 'why' a certain mathematical procedure works and not just 'how' it works; in this respect, 'why?' is the most frequently asked question in class.

4. At the end of class I summarize the new concepts and I assign homework. Occasionally I show 1-2 examples from the new homework set on the board and I offer students a chance

to ask questions on anything concerning the course.

Summary:

All work in class is being done in a lively manner and in a relaxed atmosphere. In this respect I insist on open communication among students, and between students and me. As I encourage note taking, students participate actively, in a non-threatening dialog format; often times the students are the ones who solve the problems, while I write on the board. Therefore, more often than not, including the presentation of new material, I act as an intermediary between students' thinking and the development of the solutions; at times we use calculators to check, explore or otherwise extend and use what we learn in class. This general approach creates a feeling of community as well as facilitates students' participation with a constant exchange of ideas. Very often I encourage the participation of students who hesitate to express themselves, by reminding them that all questions and suggestions are welcome. This way, students simultaneously improve their confidence and optimize their understanding of the subject matter."

With this picture in mind, I would like to elaborate on the main reasons I think an implementation of the new trends at the expense of traditional lecture will not improve students' success. In this respect, I have been receptive to the discussion around this subject, and some recent proposals seem to be prematurely offered and rarely ever necessary, except perhaps in remote areas with little or no educational infrastructures. There is no pedagogical reasoning or statistical evidence to support the conversion of developmental mathematics to group-collaborative teaching or to a software program across the board, let alone expanding such approaches to higher-level courses.

Concerns about group-collaborative strategy in teaching developmental mathematics

1. The five challenges repeatedly mentioned concerning group work are: students in groups with different ability levels, groups with inequitable participation, students working at different rates, group members causing confusion, and off-task behavior. These five problems with group learning point vehemently to the greatest and perhaps the most essential reality of human life: people are not equal with respect to abilities and many other personal traits! Forcing students to work in groups ("collaborative learning") can easily become counterproductive and even unethical: students may learn from students who are not pedagogically prepared to explain the 'why' of a math procedure since the instructor is not really teaching. The better students can become arrogant 'instructors' while others can feel humiliated (even if they don't express it), and the students who could navigate faster and easier through the material are held back, wasting precious time as they are required to complete the same amount of work at a much slower pace. Beside this, some stu-

dents don't even need to do as many repetitive exercises and "collaborative activities" as others, hence the extra waste of time and more built-up frustration.

2. The claim of better success offered by collaborative learning (let's call this course 0332) is very shaky, to say the least; the unsubstantial rate of reported 3% improvement over the traditional 0330 course at my institution should raise a multitude of questions. In fact, it may be attributed solely to these three factors: one extra hour of work per week in 0332 versus 0330 (a significant 29% increase in instruction time allotted to 0332), a high percentage of students in 0332 have already attempted 0330 (so they are familiar with the curriculum), and an alarming 30% of the final grade in 0332 is based on homework done online, quizzes online, and other unreliable assessments (group quizzes, etc.). All of these important circumstances contribute substantially to grade inflation in 0332. In fact, just one extra hour of class time per week in the traditional lecture setting will increase more substantially the rate of success in this course, much more than a mere 3%.

3. As far as human development is concerned, college students should evolve into dependable professionals able to rely on themselves to complete demanding tasks in their line of work, and to display creativity and willingness to take initiative. All of these require a high level of personal responsibility that is

not promoted by group (collaborative) learning; after all, everybody's work may turn out to be nobody's work. Indeed, such responsibility is negatively affected at the expense of dependency on the group and/or on the software involved. After all, if students are not individually well prepared, what quality contribution can they bring to a group?

4. It is obvious that the experience, expertise, and pedagogical training of the faculty are wasted within both the collaborative learning model and the software teaching. Indeed, it is the reality of this relatively new 'philosophy of education' often promoted in academic circles, 'Do not be a sage on the stage, be a guide on the side,' that should seriously concern us. In fact, the opposite is much more beneficial to our students: one should strive to learn from a sage on the stage, an experienced instructor, instead of struggling to learn something from a guide on the side, or even worse, from an unprofessional 'instructor' incarnated in a classmate who happens to be in the same group. It should be abundantly clear that such unprofessional teaching is conveying something about mathematics but not the rigorous mathematics we claim we want to teach. Via this method, excellence is sacrificed to mediocrity, and consequently, versatility in students' degree plan selection is drastically limited.

Arguments for mathematics education in classroom lecture versus education about mathematics on software.

As technology is used more and more in the teaching of mathematics, especially at the developmental level, a pejorative meaning has been unjustly associated with the word "lecture," as in "classroom lecture" offered by an experienced instructor. I say "unjustly" because those who share such an opinion seem to forget one crucially important fact: human beings learn only by some kind of lecture. In this respect, when we learn from a book, the book is lecturing us; when we learn by experience, the experience is lecturing us; when we learn from a video, the video is lecturing us; when we learn in a group, the group (or an individual in the group!) is lecturing us; when learning is mechanically guided by a preprogrammed piece of software, the software is lecturing; and so on.

Naturally then, a question arises: which kind of lecturing should we consider more appropriate for an excellent education? Although learning by experience, in a group, from a video, or on software can be additional learning avenues, they should not, for most purposes replace or be substitutes for lecture: live and professional classroom lecture should be treasured as sacred. This is the best time an experienced instructor has to manifest her/his expertise to impart to all students in the classroom personally and thoroughly the subject matter. Therefore, traditional lecture based on proven pedagogical precepts should remain the main method to deliver solid mathematics education, while non-pedagogical approaches, especially via software, should be made available as additional but optional

educational possibilities at all academic levels and outside the classroom, subject to exceptions based on lack
of educational infrastructure.

In the following I would like to randomly enumer-
ate a few reasons supporting my thesis. As far as
higher education is concerned, there are many more
life-long gains in classroom lecture than there are provided by learning on software. Some of these benefits
are: number sense, common sense, mathematical understanding, self-responsibility including time man-
agement, meaningful college experience, and readers
can provide their own in order to reinforce the pro-lec-
ture criteria.

1. As I mentioned before, good math education
   should be much more than just learning the
   concepts and how to solve a problem. The
   main focus should be on reason and logical
   understanding, as to why certain procedures
   work, rather than only what to do to find the
   answer. The instructor in the classroom can
   accomplish this goal quickly, efficiently, and
   effectively while non-pedagogical approaches may fail miserably.

2. Classroom instruction provides constructive
   live socializing time for students and instructors, traits, advantages and practices on
   the verge of extinction in an era of cellphone,
   television, calculator, and computer screen
   taking over and greatly reducing meaningful human contact and communication. Indeed, along with an increasingly accepted
   but nevertheless illusory 'social media,' a
   mathematics computer lab displays a sad

picture of separation and isolation of human beings who give in to the 'easy, simple, and less work' temptation in education, accepting to be lectured to by insensitive screens.

3. Direct interaction and communication in the classroom offer an excellent environment to enhance patience, understanding of human nature, and respect between people, which are almost completely neglected in a computer lab setup as one person on one computer, where students rarely share ideas and/or opinions with each other.

4. Open questioning is one of the most useful and effective practices in education. Not only does this offer students almost instant answers to stringent questions, but usually helps other students with similar inquiries; this happens frequently during classroom lecture, but it is missing almost completely in most computer lab settings.

5. During the sacred classroom time, instructors can effectively show the larger picture and value of what is being learned. Connections with the previous material and anticipating how and where the new concepts are being used (real life applications, for example) can be quickly presented in order to make it all more interesting and relevant.

6. In classroom lectures experienced instructors can find precious time for short philosophical discussions and wisdom stories pertaining to some mathematics concepts

such as irrational numbers, the concept of infinity, systems of equations, etc., which can open a much wider view of mathematics for the students.

7. Who wants to watch a boring show? Unlike the impersonal and boring atmosphere in most mathematics computer labs, a classroom lecture offers the ideal avenue for an exciting and entertaining "live show." Most people learn faster and easier by association, so, instructors can bring connecting humor and meaningful personal stories that can incite students' interest, making learning more fun and productive in the classroom setting.

8. It is well documented that human beings learn better in an emotionally charged atmosphere, especially as we recognize multiple intelligences. What kind of emotion does a software offer? Virtually and usually none! Instead, in a traditional lecture format, experienced instructors can bring to the classroom a sensible emotional component in order to trigger higher learning responses from students.

9. The beauty of mathematics cannot successfully be presented by dry and mechanical preprogrammed software. Instead, instructors' lectures during the sacred teaching time can show multiple ways to solve a math problem, allowing students to choose their preferred method. Such approach can help more students discover the beauty of mathematics, and hopefully convince them to

even become math teachers instead of some mere software supervisors posing as teachers.

10. Two chief claims favoring "software teaching" of mathematics are along the lines of being cheaper and faster! Indeed, it is somewhat cheaper, and students can work at their own pace, with some being able to learn faster than others. However, based on reasons listed here, it is by far not the best approach, and some researchers even call it the "McDonald-ization" of the teaching of mathematics; obviously, here comes 'cheap and fast' to replace thorough mathematics education; here comes learning something about mathematics, rather than learning why and how math works, and how to effectively use it.

Consequently, there is an imperative need for education professionals (Public Schools and Higher Education Coordinating Boards, along with accrediting agencies) to step in and reinforce a path based on rigor, logic, utility, and excellence. Such professionals should definitely know what is best for our students, and high standards should not be sold out to "cheaper and faster." After all, it is widely known that good things require time and work, while "cheap and fast" more often than not lead to mediocrity for the short term, and potential disaster for the long term. For most students, the learning of mathematics necessitates time for sufficient practice in order to properly assimilate new concepts, especially considering developmental students at community colleges who, for the most part, have never been properly taught mathematics. The well-treasured "college experience" cannot take place in front of a screen. Instead, it requires people, interaction, debate, exchange of ideas, and this naturally implies valuable time spent in a classroom lecture format. Therefore, educators should reconsider the implementation of an "accelerated" computerized methodology in the teaching of developmental mathematics. Refocusing on well-structured lecture while saving non-pedagogical educational avenues for remote locations lacking any educational infrastructure, or as additional/optional endeavors outside the classroom, will ensure readiness for our students to compete domestically and even internationally as they aspire to rewarding careers in a changing world.

References

Gene I. Rochlin, Trapped in the Net.
David Shenk, Data Smog.
Clifford Stoll, High Tech Heretic.
Irie Glajar, Teach For Life.
Jose Antonio Bowen, Teaching Naked: How Moving Technology out of Your Classroom Will Improve Student Learning.
Katheleen Almy, The Emporium Model: Not a Magic Bullet for Developmental Math.
"The Case against Computers in K-13 Math Education (Kindergarten through Calculus)" article from "The Mathematical Intelligencer" - Like a quack cure in medicine, perhaps the most harmful effect of the computer craze is that it diverts people from other,

more solidly grounded approaches to treating the ailments of mathematics education. Might not the Golly-Gee-Whiz-Look-What-Computers-Can-Do school of mathematical pedagogy eventually come to be regarded as a disaster of the same magnitude as the ``new math'' rage of the 1960s?

16

International Standards

People never improve unless they look to some standard or example higher and better than themselves.

Tyron Edwards

One could say that in order to evaluate an educational system, we should inspect its outcomes in the respective country. Since education is meant primarily to improve the lives of the graduates, a meaningful way to do this is perhaps to compare the education standards with the quality of life in countries around the world. According to some international statistics, here are the *top ten educational systems* in the world (in this order): Finland, South Korea, Hong Kong, Japan, Singapore, England, The Netherlands, New Zealand, Switzerland, and Canada. At the same time, here are the *top ten 'quality of life' countries* (not in this order): Norway, Sweden, Germany, Ireland, The Netherlands, Liechtenstein, Australia, U.S.A., Canada, and New Zealand.

With these lists in front of us we can detect several interesting facts, and here are some that I would like to discuss. There are only 3 countries that made both lists. There are no countries on either list where one of the five romance languages is predominant (Italian, Spanish, French, Portuguese, and Romanian). Note that with the obvious exception of U.S.A., Canada, and Germany, the listed countries have in general small populations. Also, most of the Western developed countries such as Austria, France, Spain, Belgium, and Italy are not on either list. In addition, notable is that the most populated countries in the world, namely China and India, are not on either list. Finally, most countries on the two lists are in the Northern hemisphere, with no countries from Africa and South America.

Of course one could find several other points of interest in comparing these two lists, but I will focus on the fact that there are only three countries placing in the top ten with respect to both criteria. This leaves seven countries where there seems to be a disconnection between education and their standard of living. On one hand such countries place high according to the quality of the educational system, but on the other they are not to be applauded for the way they use education to enhance the quality of life of their populations. By no means do I suggest that these populations live poorly, but I think that under a cause and effect scenario, more countries with good educational systems should be capable of assuring their populations respectively higher standards of living.

Also, I don't mean to suggest that the above-described reality applies only to the top ten countries in the world. Indeed, I think this discrepancy is more widespread than we would like it to be, and it manifests itself in both directions. In this respect, there are many other countries where the educational system might be highly respected while the quality of life is not commendable, and there are those nations where, even with mediocre educational systems, their populations enjoy an above average standard of living.

The question is imminent: why? Can we conclude that in fact it doesn't matter? Can we say that there is actually no real connection between the quality of education and the quality of life in the respective countries? I think that in an ideal world the two should be connected. However, in our world of such prominent variety of political systems, ethnic and cultural history, and, why not, religious backgrounds, it seems understandable to accept the mentioned disconnect.

In the end, I believe it should all be left to the discretion of the individual human beings living around the world. Whether we like it or not, one meaningful saying suggests that each nation deserves its leaders, and I would generalize this by saying that it deserves its leaders in all respects: from education and politics, to the economy and religion. The alternative – victimizing some nations but not others – is meant to take away the power of the people to craft their own avenue in life. Human history is abundant with examples where nations arrived at crossroads in their development when they had to make drastic, many times risky or even bloody choices. Nevertheless, they were able to change course for the better – see the 1989 anticommunist revolutions of Eastern Europe. Consequently, regardless of the present educational system and the quality of life a nation enjoys, there is always room for change as long as that nation desires it smartly and strongly enough. Similarly, risky or not, the same potential is available to the individual human being virtually regardless of circumstances, and this should be a personal conviction for those striving to improve their lives.

17

No Intentional Negativity

The happiness of your life depends upon the quality of your thoughts ... take care that you entertain no notion unsuitable to virtue and reasonable nature.

Marcus Aurelius

From ancient wisdom to modern self-growth programs offered by trained philosophers and psychologists, we are presented with a wide range of teachings that speak in unison: be positive, be constructive, and never pursue negative thoughts, words, or actions. Here are a couple of examples that I find very suggestive.

Regardless of one's religious beliefs, it is well known that for the most part, spiritual teachings have been promoting positivity, compassion, and personal responsibility for millennia. In this respect, the ancient Incas of South America had an abbreviated everyday three-step salute that in essence meant: work hard, don't lie, and don't make anybody suffer. This seems to portray a great picture of human behavior and participation in life that points toward the elimination of suffering, hence no negativity. Along the same lines, in his book *Jesus and Buddha; The Parallel Sayings*, Marcus Borg presents an impressive parallel between some of the consecrated sayings of Jesus, which are strikingly similar to those of Buddha. One famous teaching is, of course, "Do to others as you would have them do to you" in the words of Jesus, with its parallel by Buddha: "Consider others as yourself." Even though these are only some examples, we can witness a conscious effort on behalf of sages and cultures across time to help build a human society based on true values away from fear, hate, and war.

A Symbol of Peace

As far as our modern society is concerned, therefore, we should refrain from creating negativity intentionally in education; negativity 'on purpose' makes absolutely no sense to any logical mind that understands the cause-and-effect nature of our universe. Education, being such a paramount facet of life, should be a positive endeavor at all times. Negativity only extends the vicious cycle of 'what goes around comes around.' The message of non-negativity in education should stem from an approach based on positive contributions of the teacher, within a framework of personal responsibility on behalf of the student. Here are a few educational areas I think would benefit from such an approach especially in higher education; at the same time I think it could be implemented at all levels, considering proper adaptations.

Don't punish college students for being absent. In many situations there are very good reasons students don't attend class and 'excused absences' should be part of the vocabulary of modern teachers and educational institutions. Students should be allowed to take responsibility for their education: they should take care of the material they miss when they are absent; hence they should take charge regarding their progress in the respective course of study.

Don't punish students for being late to class: even 5 minutes of class is better than no class at all. In most cases teachers should be flexible and professional enough such that a late student doesn't disrupt the entire class activity. Students should feel welcome to class at all times but at the same time they should be made aware of the consequences class lateness would infer in their academic progress.

Don't punish students for taking their cellphone (text-messaging) emergency calls during class as long as they leave the room so as not to disturb other students, the teacher, or the general class activity. In some cases there are emergencies that students can quickly take care of in a few seconds 'on the spot.' Of course, certain rules should apply as it pertains to tests and exams.

Don't punish students for not doing their assigned homework. We need to remember that students are not of equal intellectual capacity to learn. Also modern research on 'multiple intelligences' shows that people learn differently. Therefore, we should allow students to do that part of homework, or that volume of homework they feel they need in order to be successful. Consequently, 'homework completion' should ordinarily not be used to grade students; supervised quizzes, tests, exams, and final exams should be the most important criteria.

Don't punish students for asking questions or questioning authority. The professionals they would eventually become need to be versed in engaging in discussions especially if it means debating controversial issues. What better environment to improve in this respect than a classroom full of inquisitive minds?

We see, therefore, how the overly rigid class rules in many institutions actually can stand in the way of true, complete, and responsible education of the next generations of graduates. Having in mind that they are our future, and as we strive for a better tomorrow, the idea of creating a classroom environment that excludes negative pedagogical trends becomes crucial. Let positivity, cooperation, understanding, and responsibility be the norms implemented in education, and the results will translate into a brighter future for our society.

18

Learn another Language

We can accomplish almost anything within our ability if we but think that we can!

George Matthew Adams

As we live in a world of connectivity facilitated by modern technology, we move closer and closer to a truly global economy. This virtually necessitates a global education. Therefore, it seems logical that our striving to communicate with people from different cultures should motivate us to make an effort to learn at least the basics of their languages. Nothing is more flattering than people's diligent determination to communicate with us in our own language, since their native language is different from ours. That intent clearly exemplifies the core of the subject at hand: communication between people starts with language.

And I can offer my own experience in support of this point. My 1981 escape from the totalitarian communist regime of Romania took me through what at that time was Yugoslavia, another member of the Eastern European Communist Bloc. However, our neighbor to the West was privileged with much more freedom than the rest of those countries, so it was easier for escapees, once in Yugoslavia, to find their way to the true freedom of Western Europe. Italy and Austria were the well-known gateways to the West, but not knowing the respective languages would have made it harder for anyone to pass through. In my case, in Yugoslavia I managed to get by with the little German I knew and once in Italy my broken English assisted me at first. However, my efforts to learn Italian while in Italy were royally rewarded by a sincere appreciation from all the friends I made over my four-and-a-half-month stay in the refugee camp of Latina, Italy.

It is true that as it stands today, English and Spanish are the two languages competing for the number one spot as the most popular language in the world. Consequently, most travelers tend to learn English or Spanish while they make travel plans for trips around the world, whether their trips are to the Americas, Europe, Asia, etc. However, this does not undermine my argument that while in France, Italy, or Germany, for example, would be nice to at least attempt to have a basic conversation in the native language with a cab driver, a restaurant waiter, or a travel agent. That effort in itself would instantly bring people closer, which implicitly will open up new avenues for a deeper, more appreciative and personal experience while abroad.

Not only that, but learning another language allows one to exercise new areas of the brain, which is a known stimulant for those people inclined to expand their intellectual horizons. It is biologically documented that the more brain cells are fired up, the more neuronal connections are established and that substantially enhances one's problem solving ability.

Irie in Sibiu, Romania

In this respect, learning another language can help understand at least some traits of people from other cultures. Moreover, the learning of another language is always paired with a study of different philosophies of life including different customs and behaviors. This way we can peacefully bridge different nationalities under the common sense understanding of what unites us instead of building more animosity on what divides us. Such an outcome can definitely help the human race solve some of its most stringent local and international problems, leading to a world-wide community that lives in unity toward common goals: wellbeing, peace, and happiness for all. In the end, we do need to realize that in fact WE ARE ALL ONE.

19

Education by Traveling

The only thing that keeps a man going is energy. And what is energy but liking life?

Louis Auchincloss

Ever since I can remember, I enjoyed traveling. It seemed that every time I left the familiar surroundings, I was on an adventurous exploration. As I was growing up in Romania in my father's native village, since my mother's family lived about 60 miles away, we were visiting them at least once a year. Traveling by means of public transportation in the 1950s and 1960s Romania was decent, but many a time would attract significant, although unpredictable elements. From trains out of schedule, to broken buses, I was in for an essential lesson in my life: waiting patiently.

The story continued and it was complemented by my 4-year daily bus commute to my high school: six times a week (sometimes twice a day), since the working/school week in Communist Romania was a six-day week. It was just about 6 miles each way but under those circumstances, especially over the 3-4 months of, at times, heavy snowy winter, the short trips had the potential of trying our young ability to handle adverse conditions, and indeed, they often did.

Then, after the 9-month mandatory military service with its own traveling trials and tribulations, came a 4-year higher education program at Babes-Bolyai University of Cluj, Romania, about 200 miles away from home. The 2-3 times a semester trips to visit my family were not without excitement. Caring heavy luggage on crowded trains was the norm, and I got used to it as time was taking me through my cherished college years. Moreover, my college volleyball playing in the first Romanian division offered the ideal opportunity to travel for free all over the country, as we were playing a variety of teams. Some of those trips were real mind openers for me since I had the rare chance to visit unique historical places, and I treasured every minute of it.

However, as extensive and educational my traveling around the country became at that point, it was all happening within the Romanian borders. I even worked for two years as a university graduate and I had not yet secured a trip to another country. As much as I was longing for it, the possibility of visiting, for example, a country in Western Europe was virtually nonexistent. The Communist regime of Romania and the Securitate (the Romanian version of the KGB, the Secret Police) made sure that people did not get a real sense of what life in freedom was. The heavy censorship was therefore also directed toward prohibiting Western goods inside the country, those available being mostly on the black market at exorbitant prices.

Within this scenario, in 1981 I took the rare chance I was finally offered to spend a 2-week vacation in Yugoslavia, with the unspoken plan in my mind to escape to the West. Once in Yugoslavia, I risked it all, and at the end of a pretty adventurous clandestine trip by train, one night I crossed the border into Italy. After a four-and-a-half month stay in the United Nations sponsored Italian political refugee camp of Latina, in 1982 I finally arrived in the U.S. as a permanent resident (full details are available in my 2012 autobiography, *Escape to Freedom*).

One can then see how my traveling for 26 years within the Romanian borders evolved into international traveling and it did it with a big bang: my first airplane flight, and it had to be across the Atlantic Ocean. Since then to the present, I have traveled to many countries both on the American and the European continents, and the experiences accumulated over the years have changed my life definitely for the better.

Teotihuacan, Mexico

The avenue of achieving this kind of transformation could not be accomplished or replaced by anything else. One could read or watch videos about other countries, other people, and other cultures, but until one sets foot on the ground in such places the experience is only theoretical. In other words, we need to savor the new through all our senses in order to let it sink into every cell of our being. That is a true human transformation, and with it comes the realization that we as individuals are not the center of the universe, and consequently, we should not take things for granted. This is real education and that is why I speak so loudly in favor of traveling as a form of practical illumination relative to the realities of our world. Of course, not everyone can afford extensive international traveling, and some people are simply not inclined to pursue it even if they could afford it. That is all understandable. However, I do suggest that people who at least get out of their familiar surroundings to near-by neighborhoods, to near-by cities, parks, or another U.S. state are much better off than those who don't. One sensitive saying recommends that every year we should visit at least one place that we have never seen before. Only by following this suggestion we can really attest to its veracity. Indeed, there is so much history, culture, and social value to every place, that only if we are there we can make it a real part of our true perception of the world.

Traveling is the best education one can get. More so, traveling to countries where English is not the primary language and where we can let ourselves be absorbed by different cultural and religious traditions, is the apogee of learning on the road. Such experiences will never be forgotten and we will never be the same afterwards. They will mark us for the rest of our lives and will make us better human beings as we make an effort to become true citizens of the world. In this respect, I would like to recount some of my deepest educational experiences while traveling.

Porto, Portugal

One such example comes from the 1970s. As mentioned before, the athletic side of my college years in Romania took me all around the country. One particularly interesting city was Suceava. Our long bus ride on a cool Saturday still left enough leisure time that day in Suceava, so we all spread around the city according to our preferences. Mine was to visit (for the first time in my life) the ruins of the impressive fortress built in the 14th century and inhabited by one of the most notorious Romanian defenders against the expansion of the well-known Turkish Empire, Stefan the Great. Indeed, per historical records preserved over time, for many years he was able to keep his country, then the Principality of Moldova, free, and his heroism became legendary. As I was walking on the same grounds he stepped on hundreds of years before, visiting chamber after chamber, I was visualizing his imposing figure marching in front of his court. Although he built 44 churches (one after every victorious war), his personal life was not up to par. Among other things, he was known to have had many illegitimate children and this fact hunted him throughout the centuries. In spite of it, in 1992, the Christian Orthodox Church of Romania decided to canonize him for his great contribution to the autonomy from the Turkish Empire, which implicitly meant saving the Christian church of Moldova from the expansion of Islam. I have never understood how sanctifying Stefan was a good choice, having in mind the moral standards the church generally promotes. We can see, therefore, how an educational experience from a 1970s travel adventure connects with more recent realities, in order to make sense and raise meaningful questions about historical and current events.

A second example of a great educational traveling experience is one of my several visits to Italy after my escape from Romania in 1981. From Latina, one can see in the distance, on top of well-eroded ancient Italian near-by mountains, the beautiful silhouette of the small town of Norma with some visible stone ruins right on a cliff of the mountain. Ever since my 1981 stay in the Latina refugee camp I longed to explore that place, but I didn't make it until this visit, a few years later. This time I was determined to step on the stone walls of Norma in person, and I did.

Norma, Italy

The ruins were totally fascinating, but untouched by independent explorers or by the Italian department of archaeology. Among huge walls made of giant blocks of stone and a gate-like entrance that closely resembled those of Cusco of Peru in South America, there I found six circular holes in the ground (arranged in two parallel rows of three), each 3-4 feet in diameter and about 30 feet away from each other. I curiously looked inside one of them (some were almost completely covered by grass) and I couldn't believe my eyes: it was 25-30 feet deep and about 15-20 feet wide. That triggered my curiosity to the max and later on that day I returned with a heavy rope. Employing an old trick I learned in my childhood, with a strong wooden pole across the hole, using the rope, I lowered myself 5-6 feet into the underground cavity and I was perplexed: I felt I was inside a giant clay pottery meant as a storage vessel of some kind. The walls of the "vessel" were smooth, just like those of a large clay pot, gently curving to the bottom, and on the floor there was a pile of dirt mixed with a few small tree branches and some plastic and glass containers obviously thrown there over the years by careless people. Reluctant to go all the way down, I pulled myself up, and I inspected the surroundings one more time. As I was walking around within the breathtaking majesty of the walled-in giant courtyard, a series of thoughts ran through my head: since the Italian government did not initiate any official archaeological effort up to that point at this site, it must have been of no interest due to its non-Roman pedigree. But that could mean it was even older, probably Etruscan, or, older still! In the end, I walked out through the breath-taking giant gate and suddenly I met an old man, a local inhabitant it seemed, dressed in working clothes and wearing a straw hat as protection against the strong Italian sun that had already visibly marked his face. Even though my Italian language ability was relatively limited, I engaged him in a conversation about the ruins, and he blew me away! He said that some years before, while he was plowing the ground to make his vegetable garden, close to the Cusco-like walls in front of us, he uncovered a few giant bones that shockingly appeared to be human but of much larger size! However, he did not say whether he reported his finding to the authorities.

Then he told me about some local legends that mentioned a human population of giants living in the area in times immemorial, much like the Bible speaks of giants who lived on Earth thousands of years ago. Wow! Have I just lowered myself with a rope down in a storage vessel that many thousands of years ago was just part of a giant cellar of six? My mind was racing as I thanked and said goodbye to the old man, and the story of the ruins of Norma stayed with me ever since.

And here is one last example of an educative experience while traveling: my visit to Romania in 1989. Almost eight years after my arrival in the U.S., with my first U.S. passport in hand, I had built up the courage to visit my family back in my native country. So, in the summer of 1989 I flew to Rome. I visited my friends in Latina and, after my best friend Sergio helped me secure a car, I started my journey to Romania. First, I traversed the Italian peninsula from Rome to the Adriatic Sea. Next, I crossed the sea at night on a ferryboat, and the next morning I was on my way on a long drive through Yugoslavia and Hungary to reach Romania the following day. Along the decent but winding roads through the hills of Yugoslavia, due to some rain, I had a minor accident: I slid off the road in some bushes that actually stopped my car from rolling over a very steep cliff. I did not suffer any injuries and the engine of my car seemed to be running well except for the fuel lines on the bottom of the car: they had been cut at the impact with the bushes. It took me about five hours to fix the car, being forced to leave it in the woods as I got help from some locals who took me to the nearest town (about six miles away) to get some parts. Since I didn't speak their language, we communicated with each other using a few words in both Italian and English. Upon our return to my car, one of the men acted as a mechanic and connected back the fuel lines. I gave them a little money and while I was taking off, I instantly became very appreciative of the Yugoslavian people in that area and especially the three men who volunteered to help me. The rest of the month-long car trip to Romania and back to Italy was apt to reinforce my belief in the intrinsic goodness of human beings and consolidated it into a firm conviction. In this respect, I was fortunate to pass through many and varied experiences that, according to the circumstances, took me up and down on the scale of my appreciation of real human values regardless of where I happened to be.

The Holocaust Memorial, Berlin, Germany

Consequently, looking back over many of my trips, I cannot but suggest once again that traveling is the best education. From Alaska and Canada to Mexico, and from England to Greece and Turkey, the many places I visited over the years had the educational quality one can only find by physically stepping onto the streets and sidewalks, or climbing up and down the well-warn stairways of ancient ruins. In addition, communicating with people from different cultures has opened my eyes to the realization of our real place on this planet, a place of unity and connection, which can help us all live in harmony. That is why I would like to encourage all readers, according to their possibilities and their inner drive, to travel as much as possible, in a pleasant and educational effort to know the world and themselves better.

20

Fearless Academic Freedom

The only thing we have to fear is fear itself – nameless, unreasoning, unjustified terror, which paralyzes needed efforts to convert retreat into advance.

Franklin Delano Roosevelt

It is my observation that real academic freedom is being gradually restricted by implementation of a variety of regulations and demands set up by departments in academic institutions all around the U.S., if not around the world. Fear of repercussion is the main reason why even senior faculty members are reluctant to speak their minds on issues affecting the integrity of teaching.

In this respect I can speak from my experience, but first I would like to remind the reader that I was born, I grew up, finished college, and worked for a couple of years in a communist country, Romania. I escaped that totalitarian regime in 1981, eight years before the anti-communist revolutions sweep of Eastern Europe, but by then my psyche was already infected by the communist propaganda with fear of free and honest speech. Of course, suppressing anti-communist political expression was 'justified' in the eyes of the Communist Party. Such expression was declared unpatriotic, since the party overly worried of losing its dominion of the country, so, freedom of expression was drastically censored in virtually all walks of life. But there were even deeper and long-lasting effects that would impregnate people's subconscious minds, as they feared instant criticism, ridicule, and punishment up to torture or prison time culminating possibly with losing their lives.

My close to home realization of this reality was once again confirmed almost as soon as I stepped on Western soil. I then better understood how far behind, with respect to courage to exercise free expression is concerned, an overwhelming majority of us, people raised under a communist flag, were. For many years after my arrival in the United States, as I was building up my teaching career in mathematics, I 'suffered' a chronic reluctance to express myself in public, especially in math departmental meetings, conferences, and workshops. There have been academic issues on which I would have liked to offer my opinion, but something in the back of my mind would stop me; it was the preconditioned fear I had subconsciously stored over all the years of communist brainwashing and propaganda infiltrated in every fiber of our beings by a totalitarian regime only interested in crushing any free expression attempt that disagreed with their agenda. So, as I was about to raise my hand to offer my ideas, many times a rush of blood in my head would promptly bring in the preconditioned response: "Watch out. What will they think of you? Do you want to be humiliated in public?" And although academic gatherings in the U.S. overwhelmingly proved to be very respectful of any member's opinion, my reluctance persisted until I fully realized that in fact faculty should speak openly within a common effort to seek better solutions for the academic issues at hand. In this respect, an extension of my understanding expanded to the general concept of academic freedom considering the actual teaching of the subject matter.

More recently, as I researched the crucially important concept of academic freedom in the United States, I discovered some of its facets that are, to say the least, intriguing. In this respect, here is what one can find in the "1940 Statement of Principles on Academic Freedom and Tenure" authored by the American Association of University Professors and the Association of American Colleges and Universities: Teachers are entitled to freedom in the classroom in discussing their subject. However, the statement also permits institutions to impose "limitations of academic freedom because of religious or other aims," provided they are "clearly stated in writing at the time of the appointment." It is also specified that the Principles are only private pronouncements but not a binding law. Moreover, as we consider limitations of academic freedom based on "other aims," I think we should be entitled to serious concern since such a statement leaves all doors open to a host of very subjective motives institutions can invoke in order to restrict faculty's freedom in teaching.

So, upon a closer scrutiny, we should ask: Is academic freedom granted to faculty, or to institutions? Can institutions dictate to the faculty what is permitted and what is not in the classroom? Must an institution ensure that individual faculty members have their pre-ferred choice of teaching? Or, is the institution, by its departments, entitled to impose on its faculty how they should express themselves academically? Moreover, should institutions sacrifice faculty's academic free-dom to the mighty (financial, and/or religious, etc.) powers of educational corporations on a mission of converting teaching from a human-to-human tradi-tional model to an approach that promotes elec-tronic/digital means in education?

And the questions continue: Should faculty fear speaking their minds on such issues? Can the constitu-tional freedom of speech right protect faculty from en-dangering their careers? All these issues are paramount as we consider the freedom of professional educators who might be negatively affected by restric-tive academic freedom. In the end, teachers want to teach their subject the best they can and according to their teaching philosophy; to a majority of us mathe-matics teachers our students' learning does matter and we do care how well they understand concepts and procedures.

Yes, changes in the education field do take place, but the subject matter remains virtually constant. This is true more so in mathematics education, a subject with which I am most concerned and do not want to see marginalized or subjected to error. At the under-graduate level, much of mathematics remains the same. The traditional chalk-on-the-board in a profes-sional lecture format style is by far still the teaching of choice at most prestigious and excellent colleges and universities around the world, as most students still appreciate an inspiring presentation by an experienced 'sage on the stage' who captivatingly opens their minds to deep meanings of the subject. After all, an overwhelming majority of us, active mathematics instructors in 2015, are the product of this approach proven to be successful over and over again for at least a century. The alternative is the watered-down teaching via preprogrammed impersonal software programs that teach something about mathematics but little about the real feeling of mathematical thinking and its application in life. As most professional educators can testify, such feeling can better be supplied in person, eye-to-eye, in a sensitive and sensible close classroom environment where students and teachers feel and relate to each other as true human beings on a great educational path together. So, should faculty speak up against outsourcing math teaching to non-pedagogical and unproven avenues especially in higher education? Should faculty be protected by academic freedom and freedom of speech in order to preserve the real meaning of education? I think they should.

Other questions arise: Should consecrated higher education faculty profess in fear of institutional repercussion if they speak their minds to support quality of teaching in their own field? Isn't such fear a slippery slope in a wrong direction for quality education? True academic freedom should provide the solution. There should be no fear for experienced faculty to express themselves in matters of teaching integrity. Not in a democracy supported by a meaningful constitution. A proven methodology to provide high quality education to our students does matter. In this respect, more and more educators should raise their voices as they each see fit, by exercising their freedom of speech in conjuncture with academic freedom in order to offer better chances that all future generations of students reach high educational standards required to stay competitive on increasingly demanding national and international markets.

21

A Vision for the World

At a deep molecular level science tells us we are made of the same stuff, we are all one, we are star-selves.

Carl Sagan

Love unites, while hate divides. It is almost as simple as that, and we know it. Over the centuries, there have been many political and religious congregations in the world that practiced the mantra 'divide and conquer' and there are still many today. From the Roman and Turkish Empires and the Inquisition, to the totalitarian communists of the last one hundred years, on their pursuit for power and domination, dictators in the state and/or the church fought hard to eliminate love and to replace it with fear, hate, senseless competition, and punishments. The results are obvious. It appears that "There's no love in the heart of the city," as a song says, there is no love in the country, and there is widespread discord in the world. One simply has to follow the headlines and this picture is sadly available.

However, I would like to say that in spite of such seeming reality, there is hope and there is love, and headlines might not be representative. Maybe positive headlines have not yet reached a 'critical number' or amount (that number or amount that may implicitly indicate or determine the entire human species' ability to practice love as a natural existential condition). And here is where we come in. One great saying states that "you cannot ask people to give you what they don't have," and that is perfectly true. In this respect, a quick look over the known history of the human race might offer the ultimate solution.

In its infancy, in order to survive, the human civilization depended almost exclusively on the existing natural unaltered environment. Over time, it learned to cultivate the soil and to treasure the animals as sustainers of life. There was an implicit respect and love for plants, for example, and people did not abuse their grace. Such relationship was made famous by the civilizations of the Native Americans and many others around the world. One can say, of course, that this was necessary in the past, but today humans have better ability to sustain themselves via technological advancements. That might be true to some extent but we need to remember that food, shelter, and clothing are still produced largely on natural principles. According to some statistics, a suggestive example comes to mind: if all bees were to be eliminated from the face of the Earth, a process already started by extensive and/or unwise use of pesticides, chemicals, wireless communication, and other abusive practices against nature, humans could perish in about four years. In this respect, regarding natural principles, many of us opt for whole foods and comfortable custom homes instead of genetically modified plants and animals, or costly impersonal mansions and/or cheaply built houses.

On such principles I would like to propose a vision of the world that may gradually eliminate hate and fear in favor of love, compassion, and patience. The model clearly springs from the evolution of human beings and human love for that which is natural or experientially learned, so that we can call it "a return to better and better." More love for vegetables, flowers, animals, fish, trees, and human beings as it all evolves for the better, should be the first step on the higher awareness ladder of our connection with the environment. Indeed, the oxygen we inhale is produced by the vegetable kingdom while carbon dioxide is used in the process. As soon as we can afford it, we should consider cultivating vegetables and flowers, or grow fruit trees, even if it is at a small scale. Caring about them and showing our love to such fragile forms of life opens an entire new world in our awareness. Harvesting a tomato, a pepper, or a pear from our own little garden plays a sacred role of a natural connector to our immediate surroundings. Once we savor the fresh and natural taste and smell of fruit and vegetables we grew ourselves, our entire perception of nature is altered: we no longer take them for granted, and instinctually make them an important part of who we are.

And then comes the animal kingdom. I was just a young lad when my grandmother on my father's side instilled in me one of the most crucial teachings regarding animal life when she said: "It is a sin to keep an animal without water and food!" Those words have become a solid part of my upbringing and manifested themselves every day once I started taking care of my pet dogs, cats, and homing pigeons. Indeed, our sensitivity toward animals as pets or in the wild can be nurtured by adopting such practice. We should make an effort to get closer to animals and birds whenever possible and to even make them a constant presence in our lives. This can definitely help us realize as a matter of fact that we are all interconnected with the flora and fauna of our beautiful planet, and consequently, we can change our attitude into one filled with love and concern for their wellbeing. As in my case, such transformation can be started in childhood, but it is really never too late: we are all on our own paths in our lives, so any time is a good time.

Finally, the vision for the world I propose here culminates with love for people. Our natural environment does include, and not as the least important, our fellow human beings all over the world. Regardless of gender, nationality, race, or religious beliefs, we are all connected on a round planet which is really a closed in eco system. In spite of the divergences that apparently separate us, we should grow to realize that in fact, by nurturing fear and hate, we are fooling ourselves into a false creed of separation from and domination over others. Such creed is only destructive, as we can witness in our modern world. Consequently, through education, traveling, and cultural exchange, each one of us should make a special effort toward peace, understanding, and patience to eventually reach the critical number our species needs in order to assure a compassionate love among all humans.

22

Write Your Own Song

If I were not a physicist, I would probably be a musician. I often think of music. I live my daydreams in music. I see my life in terms of music. I get the most joy in life out of music.

Albert Einstein

Write your own song, or simply put, express yourself! My love for music has been nurtured ever since I remember via my mother's musical talent manifested throughout her professional life as a kindergarten teacher. The first musical instrument I learned to play was the harmonica, an instrument my mother used frequently in activities with her young students. Within a very limited range of light radio music the Romanian Communist censorship allowed during those years, I was able to savor a small selection of some nice Italian, French, and English rock-and-roll songs that moved me early on. Cliff Richards, Remo Germany, and The Beatles come to mind.

Even though by the end of the 8th grade I had been taking French in school for four years, I wasn't really paying attention to the text of (at least) the French songs I would listen to on the radio. As soon as I started high school – described in much detail in my autobiography *Escape to Freedom* – I began listening to the underground radio broadcast from Munich, West Germany, against communism in Eastern Europe: it was the famous Free Europe Radio. Suddenly, the text of some rock-and-roll songs such as John Lennon's Imagine and Power to the People captured my attention and motivated me to study English on my own since it wasn't taught at my school. However, the four years of high school took me mostly on the wave of rock and progressive rock music, but not so much on the messages imparted by the texts, whatever the messages were supposed to be. In this respect, I taught myself to play drums, and towards the end of high school, together with a few classmates, we formed a rock-and-roll band in which I was the singer and the drummer.

Throughout college and the two years that followed, I played in Romania as I gradually improved my skills, but only after my 1981 escape from communism I became driven to write my own music. As I was teaching myself guitar while I spent four and a half months in the Italian refugee camp of Latina, I composed my first song with meaningful English lyrics that had to do with the nostalgia of leaving everything behind and facing a brand new life. Then, over many years in the freedom of the U.S.A., over a vast collection of LPs, tapes, videos, and CDs, I began selecting some of the most meaningful rock-and-roll songs meant to improve the human condition.

Consecrated artists, in their conscious effort to help the human race, have composed impressively motivating pieces of music deep enough to change one's life through their messages. I will list here some of them, in order to encourage you the reader to search for your own: Queen (Innuendo, Made in Heaven), Uriah Heep (The Wizard), Bob Seger (Lock and Load), Moody Blues (Say it With Love), Eagles (Get Over it), Rare Earth (Celebration), Scorpions (Same Sun), Ozzy Osbourne (Dreamer, I just Want You), Black Sabbath (Born Again, Computer God), Metallica (Nothing Else Matters), Jethro Tull (Wind Up), and Whitesnake (Sailing Ships).

Irie on Drums

Pairing my love for music with my long-term infatuation with personal growth, and after I played on a few improvised bands, I have constructed a platform from which I continued writing my own music, with my own lyrics as I was playing all instruments. In other words, I started my own one-man-band. This gave me total freedom in terms of musical ideas and text, and I have been very happy to be able to create my own legacy in this respect; meanwhile, I realize the amateur flavor of it from production to the actual home-studio recording. However, I consider the message of any piece of art most important. In respect to my music, some of the songs are centered on personal growth ideas, and one in particular describes the euphoria that embraced the population of Romania in December 1989 at the overthrow of the communist regime of Ceausescu.

One thing is for certain: without a doubt, we are all creative. Please don't say no, and here is why. Each one of us can find an area of our lives where we can come up with a new constructive idea: that is creativity. If you don't agree, think again. Some of us are creative on the job, some of us on family matters, some on artistic endeavors, and if some claim no creativity at all, I offer this: some of us are very creative at creating non-creativity! Seriously! Surely some of us can recreate ourselves the way we are today every day for the rest of our lives, and there is absolutely nothing wrong with that. On this theme, a clever saying states that some people live 81 years, while some live a year 81 times. How true! Therefore, I suggest we embrace and take responsibility for our lives, choosing a more and more positive attitude and at the same time make a conscious effort toward manifesting our intrinsically given share of creativity however insignificant it may appear at first.

With this in mind, in the spirit of amateurship, I would like to encourage everyone to venture into writing their own piece of music, their own meaningful lyrics, their own poem, or to write their own story. As the saying goes, don't die with the music still in you. Indeed, it would be a shame to let something valuable be lost in the unspoken anonymity of the past. Instead, let it be recorded in some form for posterity. Family members, relatives, friends, and even strangers may well appreciate your creations in ways not yet known. Along these lines I should mention the 20-minute recording my grandfather enriched us with in 1972 at my insistent request to him to sing some of the folklore he so much loved: he was singing these songs alone, or to entertain friends and family, especially while working. After all these years, beside several photos, the 20-minute audio recording is the only vivid treasure we have to remember him, and what a treasure it is; my grandfather did not die with the music still in him although he passed away two years later.

I would like to close this essay with the lyrics of a musical piece of mine, and encourage you to set yourself free to write your own poem, song, or create an original composition of any kind; it will be a precious addition to your legacy, and might help someone in ways that cannot or may not currently be experienced.

Existence

It was the morning after

The day before the birth of time,

When I realized what

I have been in the future

Of … my past existence.

Springtime blooms arrived within
My inner vision, whispering gently:
You spring, and your perennial
Spring procreates the past springs
Of … your future existence.

Dreams of the morning after
The day before time was born,
Bring subtle quantum meaning
To lives which sprung from
The future of … a past existence.

Today, the spring of dreams,
Submerged in the beautiful
Darkness of a joyful star,
Sets forth quiet longings
From … my eternal existence.

You Are
You are.
You have never been,
You will never be.

You just are.
Albert was right:
Now, and now, and now,
You just are.
Time is but an illusion,
A whisper, again and again:
You are, you are, you are.
In thought you have been.

As you think, you will be,
But you ARE, just now,
And now, and now, and now, …

23

Let the Universe Handle the Details

I take it that what all men are really after is some form of, perhaps only some formula of, peace.

James Conrad

As we look around us, we observe a multitude of situations in which people go out of their way to cause desired outcomes in their lives. Although this is basically the manner in which we accomplish our goals, I think in many cases people go too far into identifying with and/or limiting themselves to the outcomes for which they long. Consequently, especially when they don't achieve their goals or they only partially achieve them, there may be a high level of disappointment, discouragement, and even despair that might poison their lives. In order to create positive solutions to our challenges and opportunities, I propose fundamental changes to the way we choose to perceive our involvement with others in the fascinating web of relationships in which we find ourselves.

In fact, such changes have been described or suggested by seers and ordinary people for millennia, and now is the best time to implement them in order to have better chances to substantially improve our lives as well as those of others. This is not an exaggeration, as I am speaking from experience. The message is really simple: if we detach ourselves from specific outcomes, results may be better than those for which we aimed. Ever since I adopted it, it brought much peace and tranquility in my life. Releasing attachment to the results of our actions and decisions sends a crucially important message that clearly states: "I have done what I needed to do; I did the best I could, and I cannot change what I have done anymore; now I am ready and responsible for the outcomes, whatever they may be, and I choose not to struggle or act negatively in retaliation." I know that in many life-changing decisions it is easier said than done, but I want to assure you the best I can, that with practice and persistence such approaches are achievable and may produce results even better than sought.

In this respect, almost nothing can substitute for personal experience, and most of us can rely on meaningful events from our lives from which to benefit. In the following I would like to relate one of my professional teaching 'adventures' that clearly proved to me the validity of this deep philosophical and beneficial chosen attitude: consider detaching yourself from exact outcomes and let the universe handle details. In my 2008 book WE ARE ALL ONE, I called this experience "The Julee Story," and here is an edited version.

It all started during a fall semester many years ago, while I was teaching an evening College Algebra class at a small satellite campus of Austin Community College, in Austin, Texas. It happened that there were two young ladies in the class, and they were actually high school seniors taking a college course. Probably escaping the high school rigidity of dress codes and other requirements, they were coming to class in light attire and were sitting next to each other in the back of the room, which was all of no real concern to me, except that they were not fully participating in the class activities. A few weeks into the semester, one of the other students, an older gentleman who was sitting in the front row, approached me after class with a very inoffensive complaint: apparently, the two high school students were disturbing him at times. In fact I had noticed that the two young ladies were amusing themselves by writing little notes to each other, but I didn't think it was an issue worth addressing at that time. However, as soon as the gentleman complained, I was obligated to approach them. So, in relative privacy, I talked to them in very nice and polite terms. I explained that some students in the class were coming to school after a long work day and it was difficult for them to concentrate in a less than ideal atmosphere. Both ladies reacted nicely to my remarks, insisting that they didn't realize they were disturbing the class, and promised to pay more attention to this matter.

For the next few weeks things went without any similar event, but soon enough the same gentleman approached me a second time with the same complaint. Once again, I didn't find the situation as desperate as it was described, but I promised to talk to the two young ladies anew. I did, and I used the same nice and polite approach, this time even suggesting that they could sit at some distance from each other if that would help. I received the same kind of response, with the promise that it would not happen again. For the rest of the semester there were no other incidents. One of the two young ladies made a "C" and the other (let us call her Julee) made a D. A grade of D was not good enough to move up to the next course, nor was it transferable.

That was a semester when students had to evaluate their instructors (every instructor was evaluated once per academic year). Not even thinking about this incident anymore, here I was, at the end of the semester, reading the students' evaluations. Out of the entire set and for the first time in many years of teaching, I had the chance to read very negative comments from two students. They sounded like this: "This instructor doesn't know how to teach, he should look for another kind of job, he is treating us as high school students." Obviously, there was little or no doubt in my mind relative to the source of the two 'anonymous' negative evaluations. In the meantime, the evaluations were sent to my department head and division chair, and I never heard a word from either of them; probably that was because the two negative comments were such an exception to the run of my good evaluations over the years.

A few days before the starting of the following semester I received a phone call from my supervisor who offered me the opportunity to teach an extra College Algebra night course at a main campus; the original instructor whose name appeared in the course schedule had to turn it down for some reason. Of course I always welcomed such opportunities and I said yes. Here I was stepping into the classroom the first day of school, when suddenly I saw Julee sitting in the front row, right in front of my desk. This time she was impeccably dressed, very presentable under any business standards, and when she saw me entering the classroom her head fell on her arms across her desk (apparently she was working now and, of course, she had to take the course again). I didn't react in any particular way; I held my first meeting as I usually do, and at the end of class she came to me and said: "You were not supposed to teach this class." I agreed and I described briefly what had happened. She said that she was trying to take that class from somebody else, stating that she couldn't learn from me. However, due to her job schedule and special work requirements, she wasn't able to switch to a different section and she couldn't drop it. Consequently, I vowed to do anything I could to help her succeed, she promised to work as hard as possible, and we both did. For the entire semester she was very dedicated, and our teacher-student relationship was one of the best. But, when all was said and done, she was only able to make another D. We shook hands, I wished her the best next time with College Algebra, and, without an offending intent, she promised to try it again with somebody else. However, the story continues.

As I was getting ready for the start of the following semester, at the end of the break, once again I received a phone call from my supervisor offering me, surprisingly enough, an extra night section of College Algebra at the same campus—the instructor scheduled to teach that course had shockingly just passed away! Of course, I said yes, and I prepared myself to teach the new section. With only a few minutes before class time, the first day of classes, I was walking towards the respective building with my briefcase in my right hand, when I noticed a silhouette walking on the sidewalk in front of me in the same direction. It reminded me of

Julee. Soon enough, my expectation was confirmed. I turned my head and I said: "Hi Julee, how are you?" She looked at me surprised, stopped, and responded to my greetings: "Where are you going?" I told her that I was supposed to teach a class in the next building. Then she asked me what course it was, and I told her it was a College Algebra section. The intensity of the conversation was rising as she asked for the room number. When I mentioned which classroom it was, she exploded in tears, hitting the nearby wall: "Oh my God! Why is this happening to me? This is not true! I was trying to run away from you and here we are again!" At that moment I dropped my briefcase asking her if she was o.k., and I answered her question: "I don't know, but this looks like karma, Julee. You know, what goes around comes around!" (Important to note is that during all of our earlier conversations I had never mentioned her negative student evaluation from two semesters earlier, neither did I ever treat her differently than the other students.) Then we went to our classroom, we tried to find alternatives for her to take that course with somebody else, but since there were none, we vowed once again to do all we could to make it work. The semester went very well from that point of view, the teacher-student relationship improved even more, but the grade she earned at the end of the semester was yet another D. We shook hands once again in a friendly atmosphere as we said goodbye, and wished each other the best.

A few semesters later, I happened to meet Julee in the tutoring center at a different campus. I asked her if she remembered me, and of course she did. She was now in Calculus doing well.

As I believe there are no accidents in our lives, I think this is a clear example of the perfect orchestration of events on Earth, where every act will be followed sooner or later by its effects. The personal karmic pattern will implicitly direct such effects towards the right person. Julee's uncalled for negative evaluation of me as her math instructor instinctively sent her right back to me however hard she was trying to avoid it. And this happened twice, in two consecutive semesters. What is even more interesting is the fact that the course sections she had chosen to take a second and a third time were exactly the ones I was assigned to teach at the last minute. Moreover, these were the only sections she could take due to her working hours and other class schedule; to make things even more dramatic, an instructor 'had' to die for the entire scenario to fit in. I believe that this was a perfect synchronicity of events that left Julee with no other exit except for withdrawal from college, which was not ideal since her employer apparently required her to be in college in order to get her degree. Simultaneously, in spite of the fact that Julee and I were committed to do whatever needed in order to increase her chances of success, an invisible mental block had been put in place so that she could not earn a passing grade during either of the subsequent semesters.

Still, as difficult as it was for her to pass that course at that time, later on she was able to do it, and even better, she was able to complete whatever other math requirements for her degree plan. This shows that her College Algebra difficulty was just one part of the results of her previous personal choice of behavior, and not a permanent condition. This suggests that once we pass the effects of many of our deeds, we can continue on the path previously set forth, as long as we don't cause serious new negative events or even chain reactions.

The Julee story is just an example of the strategy I suggest we adopt in order to improve our lives. It seems obvious that all we need to do is be true to our purposes, do all we can to fulfill our chosen responsibilities, and reduce our attachments to the results. In an invisible way, the universe seems to take care of the details. In this respect, it is evident to me that I didn't have to do anything different in order to fix the obvious wrongs Julee did by her uncalled-for negative evaluation; somehow she may have been directed to the precise course sections to which I was assigned to teach at the last moment. As much as she was trying to run away from me, she failed to accomplish such mission. At a deeper level of reality, she was committed to balance the intended negativity she sought to inflict by her evaluation, and in the end this was accomplished with no effort on my side.

The conclusion I find imminent is that as long as we know we did the best we could to cause positive outcomes, not hurting anyone or the venue involved in the process, we should not attempt to right all wrongs even if we face some negativity along the way (who knows, perhaps, in the meantime, some negativity may play a significant role in our own growth). We should choose to believe that the universe always provides unbiased justice, and that particular awareness can grant us the energy and positive determination to continue doing what we can in all circumstances without undue attachment to the results. Such a strategy may well help us become better stewards of our planet as we aspire to higher levels of moral and ethical achievement.

24

Meditate

All the troubles of life come upon us because we refuse to sit quietly for a while each day in our rooms.

Blaise Pascal

As we search for guidance with respect to stringent questions in life, we develop a variety of personal approaches suited to our own sensibility. Regardless of the labels used in traditional science or elsewhere, one thing is clear: in order to learn, one needs to listen. Yes, the learning process is very complex and can take place on a variety of avenues (doing, memorizing, repeating, etc.), but nothing is more pertinent to learning than listening.

And by listening I don't mean only reception of informative noise. No, not at all. Listening comprises a much wider range of 'noise,' including the 'sound' of our most inner thoughts. How many times a day do we surprise ourselves having a soundless 'conversation' with ... ourselves? That's one way many intriguing intuitive thoughts make their way to our conscious scrutiny, and some contribute significantly to life-changing decisions: "Do you think I should pursue a career in Finance or in Business? I think you will be better off in

Business since your mind seems to work better that way. You know, I think you're right."

However, if we keep talking, let that be silently or loudly, we cannot listen. Indeed, the listening process is one of reception but not expression. That is when meditation comes in. To be clear, we need to understand that the word "meditate" itself encompasses a variety of meanings: we meditate when we take a walk and listen to only our steps and the sounds of nature around us; we meditate when we intently listen to a favorite piece of music; we meditate when we admire a breath-taking view of a forest, a lake, or a mountain chain, and we meditate when we engage in a repetitive task such as the uttering of a mantra (a favorite sound, word, or phrase). So, as these examples illustrate, the meditation approach is in fact the quieting of the mind by focusing on only one thought.

Yoga Meditation

This is the meditation I would like to describe as the preferred avenue to one of the most listening-conducive environments. When we can focus on one chosen thought only, by setting aside all other thoughts that are swirling in our minds, we can create a state of receptive awareness that can facilitate an optimal listening. In this respect, my favorite physical activity conducive to meditation is yoga. Since controlled breathing is an implicit component of a good yoga session, the selected sequence of asanas (yoga physical positions) embodies an ideal scenario. The various stretching stands help also to compress specific parts of the body, which is meant to activate energy centers that are otherwise dormant. Consequently, the focused concentration during each asana allows the mind to reach a level of relaxation in the silence created as we put aside all other thoughts. Such a state of mind can definitely improve listening, hence learning, which can offer optimal chances for personal growth as we seek to improve our lives.

Music Meditation

Each one of us has a favorite music style, whether that be classical, jazz, blues, rock, pop, progressive, country, or any alternatives. And if one doesn't, I suggest that they should search for one; it is never too late to select that musical harmony that brings a proper level of vibration to positively affect people's emotions. Yes, you guessed it: music can be an ideal medium for meditation. I know, because I have been using it ever since I can remember. True: at first I was listening to my favorite music intently without a 'meditative purpose.' It was just because I liked it so much; it appealed to me. But later, it became a purposefully selected avenue for relaxation, and now a fantastic mediator for meditation.

So, select a piece of your favorite music, find a quiet place you can relax, play the music and breathe deeply a few times. Then start focusing on the music *only*. Gently push all other thoughts aside by telling 'them' that you don't have the time right now. Listen intently: choose to pay focused attention to individual instruments, voices, and effects, as you follow with deep admiration the lead vocals, instrumental solos, or well-orchestrated harmonies and synergies. Savor every note, every intonation, every time-signature change, and take in their pleasant vibration. Not only can this supply you with a deep sense of satisfaction, but it will also allow your mind to focus on *only* one thought: your favorite music. Well-rehearsed, such a meditative practice can offer an endless source of rejuvenation and reenergizing as you need it in your life.

The chakras meditation

In closing I will present yet another approach to meditation, perhaps one that is closer to the traditional understanding of the word, and I call it 'the chakras meditation.' This is a sequence of steps meant to help us reach that deep state of relaxation needed for listening, and it is based on the 7 energy centers that correspond to the 7 endocrine glands in the human body, as Shirley MacLaine emphasizes so well.

Step 1: Find a quiet place where you will not be disturbed by others or by loud noises. Sit comfortably in a chair or stretch out on a couch or on the floor. You might want to peacefully look into the light of a small candle (scented candles, if you prefer) or just close your eyes. Start by focusing your attention on your breath; breathe completely by inhaling deeply as you allow the air to fill up your lungs from top to bottom. You might want to count your breathing: 1-2-3-4 seconds to inhale, 1-2 seconds to hold, and 1-2-3-4 seconds to exhale. After about 7 complete breathing cycles you can move to step 2.

Step 2: Breathing freely, now you are ready to count yourself up from 1 to 7 as you focus your attention on the respective chakras and colors (please see the list a few pages ahead). Take about 7 seconds to visualize each number and location colored in and surrounded by its color while you repeat the number and this autosuggestion in your mind: "This energy center is very well balanced." Here are the numbers with their energy centers (chakras) colors and their location in the body: 1 – red - at the bottom of the spine, 2 – orange - in the sexual organs area, 3 – yellow – in the abdominal area, 4 – green – the heart area, 5 – blue – the throat area, 6 – indigo – the middle of the forehead area, and 7 – violet – the very top of the head.

Step 3: Now repeat this sentence slowly several times in your mind: "I am completely relaxed." Then you can start making the pre-selected autosuggestions (whatever you intend to improve or reaffirm in your life). Here is a possible version: "I am healthy, I am young, I am strong, I am loving, I am harmonious, I am happy and I am successful." You can also create a circle of love in your mind where you can 'invite' others to have a healing conversation, or you can hold a peaceful period of silence in which you pay attention to your breath only and you may want to slowly repeat while you inhale-exhale: "Rising-Falling." That is an effective setup for an ideal listening period since you put aside all other thoughts. You may even want to welcome intuitive input by repeating: "I am open to receive positive suggestions." Then just listen patiently to any ideas or messages that might surface in your relaxed mind; remember, it is you who decides how you receive them and what you may do with such information. After all, some of the answers surfacing at this point might be the proper response to your on-going inquiries.

Step 4: When you decide to end your meditation you count yourself down from 7 to 1 by following Step

2 in reverse. Along the way, repeat the following sentence to yourself a couple of times: "When I get to 1 I will feel rested, I will be awake, energized, ready, and relaxed." As soon as you get to 1 you may want to express your gratitude for a good meditation session simply by uttering a soft whisper: "Thank you."

For the sake of clarity, I include here a listing of the seven chakras and their colors:

VIOLET	7	THE CROWN CHAKRA
INDIGO	6	THE FOREHEAD CHAKRA
BLUE	5	THE THROAT CHAKRA
GREEN	4	THE HEART CHAKRA
YELLOW	3	THE ABDOMINAL CHAKRA
ORANGE	2	THE SEXUAL ORGANS CHAKRA
RED	1	THE EARTH CHAKRA

25

Identify Patterns in Life

What can any of us do with his talent but try to develop his vision, so that through frequent failures we may learn better what we have missed in the past.

William Carlos Williams

Identifying patterns in people's lives can help find reasons for certain decisions that might not make full sense at first glance. Understanding patterns can bring peace of mind away from regrets or self-punishment. Are we constantly rushing? Do we always get into the same kinds of relationships, whether those be mundane friendships or of a more intimate nature? Do we always let others lead while we always follow? Do we find ourselves unconditionally loving the world around us, or do we always want it to be different? In a universe governed by cause-and-effect, patterns must have causes, however subtle such causes might appear; indeed, they could be of a much deeper nature than ever expected. In 2012 I completed my autobiography *Escape to Freedom*. As I was looking back over some of the most significant events in my life and the lives of those around me, I was pleasantly surprised to find significant patterns that now, in retrospect, help me see events in a completely different light. And, I must add, this realization often puts a smile on my face–a smile of acceptance, understanding, and peace of mind.

Here is a clear example of a life-changing pattern in my father's life, of which I wasn't aware for years. It wasn't until the end of my high school experience when my father shared with me a number of 'secrets' from his own past. As he was helping me get ready for university life, he found the proper time and place to unveil some of the events that seemingly guided him in directions he never wanted to follow. He patiently described the circumstances that led him to make the decision, which created a domino effect life-changing pattern. While in his senior high school year, three years after the drastic totalitarian communist takeover in Romania, he joined an anticommunist group of students from the city of Fagaras where he was going to school. Full details are presented in my autobiography so I will focus here only on the events pertinent to the theme at hand.

Captured by the Securitate, he was sentenced to one year in prison. That derailed his path to university studies, although he was an exemplary math and science student. However, once freed from prison he worked and studied to get his high school diploma, and then applied to several universities in Romania. He aced every admission examination but in spite of that, he was repeatedly rejected since he was on the black list of the new regime: the Securitate would not tolerate students nurturing anticommunist sentiments, especially in higher education.

So, here comes the first step in a remarkable pattern: still in love with academics, my father decided to apply to the only other higher education institution left outside the eye of the Securitate since it wasn't under the traditional Ministry of Education. That was Theology. Although his heart was in math and sciences, he had to settle for a field of little or no previous interest to him, and that again because he loved books. However, as he pursued this path, he promised to himself that yes, he will graduate but he will only accept work as a librarian; he could not see himself preaching in a church even though he will actually be trained to become a Christian Orthodox priest. Time passed, he graduated, he got married, and here comes the second step in the pattern: he was not able to secure a librarian position anywhere in the area. Pressed by family responsibilities, he had virtually no choice but to accept a priest job. In the process of finding an opening, he said to himself: anywhere but not in my hometown. It was an ardent and prolonged search, and, get ready for the third step in the pattern, the only parish that became vacant was in his (our) hometown. The rest is history.

We can see, therefore, how a decision can gear one's life into an undesired direction, which eventually can start a pattern hard or even impossible to escape. In my father's case, he understood the complexity of the entire sequence of events, and that gave him the peace of mind that allowed him to accept all the ups and downs that colored his life. However, all patterns should serve positive purposes. If by their nature they help us live a happy, helpful, and fulfilled life, we should treasure them. On the other hand, if patterns show that we are repeatedly running into situations seemingly not of our choosing, they should help us take charge as long as we desire a change. So, either way we look at patterns, we should see them for what they are: windows into our lives. Through such windows we can 'see' why certain events happen, and, at least we should be better able and motivated to select the choices that allow us to change circumstances that we don't particularly like. Ultimate outcomes and results known and unknown may be better than we could have even imagined.

As another example, here is a special pattern that has been taking place with impressive frequency in my own life. Over the years I realized that as a general rule, most negative events or undesired news came into my life with no warning. And here is what I mean. Most people, as they face some negativity, are able to say: I knew it, or I was afraid of that. In my case it seems that any significant negativity, including, what we consider, really bad news, often comes at a moment's notice. In most cases, I don't entertain any thoughts about the respective events, and then … boom, they suddenly appear (a clear example is my father's unexpected passing in April 2012). After a while, I learned to use this pattern to release the implicit anxiety and pain immediately following such events. Sometimes, as soon as it happens, I can even find a self-assuring smile on my face while I take appropriate action; it is my own way to say: here it is again, deal with it. At the same time there is a reverse pattern in my life: those undesired possibilities that I sometimes entertain and I dread in my mind, often never take place; of course, as I put them aside, I say to myself: to worry is useless, and this most likely will not happen at all. In the end, my awareness of these patterns helps me better handle moments when otherwise I would blame external matters rather than take responsibility. In addition, I usually avoid being tempted to express fear and regrets, or entertain self-punishing thoughts.

Consequently, I hope we can all identify patterns that could help us make more sense even of life-turning events that might appear at first as negative. It should all be used to bring more peace of mind and understanding that can definitely help us improve our lives. On an even larger scale, as we share it, this awareness can help others on their evolutionary paths toward a better future.

26

The Person Sanctifies the Place

A wise man turns chance into good fortune.
Thomas Fuller

Some years ago I encountered this version of an anonymous wisdom story that expressively illustrates this title: A man buys a small piece of cheap land, full of rocks, weeds, wild bushes, and half-dead trees. The man loves his land and, in a couple of years of persistent and dedicated hard work, he turns it into a beautiful vegetable and flower garden. Soon enough, an old friend of his pays him a visit and exclaims: "Wow! What a beautiful garden God blessed you with!" To this, the man responds: "Yes, but you should have seen this place when God had it all to himself!"

Along these lines, as I look back over my youth in Romania, I would like to say that the totalitarian communist propaganda did not work well to convince people of the paramount importance of personal responsibility and the value of exercising one's choices in life. 'Choices' made by the communists were meant such that people lived within the confines of very limited options to improve their lives. Once it became a reality that in fact they did not own anything anymore

since virtually everything in the country had been nationalized, most people lost their inner motivation for
improvement as far as the state property was concerned.

However, the situation was quite different at family level. The few possessions people still had around
their household became increasingly valuable. Over
my teenage years spent with my parents and grandparents, this reality was abundantly clear to me: we
treasured everything we had almost as gold. My
grandparents especially were notorious at this. They
made every effort to keep agricultural tools working as
long as possible and they took great care of their life
sustaining farm animals since we were living in a small
village. And their attitude spilled over to me also.
Within that environment, I learned one important lesson: whatever you do, wherever you are within the immediate family reach, do something to improve it.

For many years now, I have been improving and
expanding my chosen attitudes. Once I escaped from
Romania of 1981 to the freedom of the U. S. and I became convinced of the unity of all things in the universe and especially in our world, the idea of
improving conditions came to me most naturally. Or
in other words, I adopted a popular philosophical
principle: whatever the conditions are when you arrive, improve them by the time you leave. Indeed, such
positive changes might include good chances that im-
provements may continue for a long time.

That is exactly what the man from our anonymous
story did. So, metaphorically, the person is destined to
sanctify the place, and with this conviction deep in our
characters we can truly embrace the message Gandhi

crafted with such wisdom: be the change you want to see in the world. Therefore, let us be the changes for good, for peace, for health, prosperity, and for love, while we strive to significantly improve our life sustaining surroundings. In the implicit unity of the world, by extension, such aspirations will contribute greatly to the betterment of the entire human race for a long time to come.

27

The Wrong Compassion

The longer we dwell on our misfortunes, the greater is their power to harm us.

Voltaire

I remember from my elementary school years many a situation when classmates were 'helping' each other feel better about not doing our homework. We were expressing some sort of compassion by saying: "Oh, don't worry, I didn't do it either!" At some level of school duty logic and group thinking, we meant to say that it was all o.k. and that, in the spirit of camaraderie, "you are not alone, so welcome to the club."

Such scenarios might appear harmless in the early stages of life, but in the long run they can help create perennial bad habits. In fact I do witness what I call "wrong compassion" in many encounters in my life. Over time, I have been making a conscious effort to eliminate my own wrong compassion practice once I understood its negative implications. And I believe there are such implications when people feel encouraged by 'compassionate' others, even though they know they are on a less than optimal path. Along these lines, some paths come to mind: procrastination, lack of physical exercise, being overweight, smoking, excessive drinking, unbalanced eating, drug abuse, egotism, jealousy, cheating, discrimination, excessive impatience, reckless driving, lack of rest, and other examples of choosing to ignore one's own responsibilities as far as striving for a better life is concerned.

But don't take me wrong: I am recognizing here two kinds of compassion. I do believe that constructive compassion is paramount to human relationships since I am convinced of the universal connection and interdependence of all that is, especially between human beings. So, what I mean by "wrong compassion" is that kind of interaction between people that encourages blame, helplessness, and standards even less than mediocre in one's life. Perhaps unintentionally, some people try to help as they 'lend a hand' by rending less-than-desirable conditions acceptable just because many others are sharing them. Such really enabling and persistent 'compassion' is only doomed to set individuals and, by extension, future generations up for failure by promoting beliefs which disempower them even when they do want to change for the better. On the other hand, true compassion may help people pull themselves up by showing trust in their ability to resolve whatever negative patterns in which they find themselves. In this respect, a compassionate human being may recognize needs of others, and acts appropriately that they gain a chance to improve their predicament. In the end, isn't that part of the ultimate goal of nurturing human relationships?

Consequently, we should do the best we can to distinguish between wrong compassion and the truly constructive kind by bringing our awareness to those sensitive encounters with people we want to help especially when they ask, and we should be cautious about any offering or giving unrequested advice. Such awareness coupled with any subsequent action can provide others the extra boost they need in order to overcome their undesired circumstances as they escape a current or potentially crippling misery.

28

Make Mondays Fridays

We are not troubled by things, but by the opinion which we have of things.

Epictetus

After a quick look around, perhaps worldwide, we easily notice that most people cherish Fridays at the expense of any other day of the week. This reality seems to be justified by the general appetite for the leisure time of the weekend, which may become the most favored time of the week by far. A clear example of such a state of affairs is my experience as a teacher in the classroom on Monday mornings: most students seem to be down and depressed, as they force themselves to function even though at a perceived low level of energy.

Along these lines, alarming statistics in the U.S. from about 20 years ago caused me to rethink my entire perception of time as we spread it over the week. The statistics showed that the number of people who die of heart problems peaks between 8 and 9 a.m. on Monday mornings. Wow! That was really startling. The obvious question is then, why? Why do more people die of heart problems on Monday mornings than any other time during the week? Not only that, but the timing seems even more precise: between 8 and 9 a.m.!

As I have been contemplating this interesting finding and as I consulted with others, it seems safe to assume that major factors, which could lead to such a reality involve one's choices as to attitudes, actions, and ways of thinking. People who suffer from some level of heart disease are more likely to cause their bodies to give up by the power of autosuggestion. The self-discourse in such cases might sound like this: "Oh God! It is Monday morning again. The weekend is over. Another week of work is ahead of me. I hate Mondays!" As we can see, this tirade of chosen, seemingly unchangeable, negative thoughts cannot but help cause human brains to send the respective messages to the corresponding organs in the body. The peptides by which the brain communicates with the rest of the human organism take the precise message of discord entertained by that person directly to the organs responsible for the vital functions in question. Consequently, a weak heart may be instantly affected by the negative thoughts and, if it is at an advanced enough phase of deterioration, it can easily succumb to the implicit message: "I hate Mondays; I wish I was dead!"

With this scenario in mind, what should we do to prevent unnecessary depression, sadness, and suffering or even death on Mondays? It seems reasonable to think that simple but profound changes in attitude may help. Why not use the power of suggestion in a positive way instead of having it cause pain and possible disaster? The energy spent to entertain negative thoughts can be redirected to send positive messages to our brains especially on Monday mornings. As soon as we convince ourselves that in many cases it is the mind that helps dictate reactions in the body, we should be free to focus our thoughts to benefit our being instead of allowing it to fall at the mercy of desperation. In this respect, a main part of what we can consider doing is to no longer give in to negative thoughts, and, instead, make conscious choices to select positive attitudes as we see ourselves in charge of everything we are doing.

One might say that this is easier said than done, but I would argue that with a little training it can be accomplished. As with everything else in life, a persistent practice will take us where we want to be. Considering my depressed students on Monday mornings, I propose to them, half-way jokingly of course, to change the names of the days of the week: Monday will be called Friday #1, Tuesday will be called Friday #2, and so on, so we can all be happy every day of the week as we are on Fridays – 'and happy hour starts every day at 4:30 p.m.' Consequently and seriously, the first step in order to change a pattern of negative thoughts into positive ones, is to examine them first; in other words, to become aware of them. As soon as we do this, we are in a position of changing them by gently saying to ourselves: "No, I don't have time for you now; I have a better thought in mind!" That allows us to 'bring in' the positive, while we choose to see the beauty of being alive in a world of opportunities. The result is that purposely-selected positivity will already occupy our mind, setting negative thoughts aside. This will surely lead to the much-desired happiness and wellbeing. In the end isn't this one of our main goals?

I think it is, and it can be reached by focused attention, intention, and practice.

29

Hobbies

That man is happiest who lives from day to day and asks no more, garnering the simple goodness of a life.

Euripides

Let's begin with this suggestion: make your work - your life sustaining activity – one of your most enjoyable hobbies. By this I mean to select as your trade that what makes you happy and fulfilled. After all, what is the alternative? Is it to do something for the rest of your life and be unhappy or even miserable? I don't think so. I would like to postulate that as long as you do with persistence and conviction that what you cannot wait to do every morning, the positive outcomes will follow, including the money. Indeed, wherever we look we find examples of people who have found what they really like doing for a living, and with patience, persistence, education, and determination they made it into a successful endeavor. After all, the love and passion you put in what you do translates unmistakably into a positive reception from those you serve, hence success.

As you pursue this worthy goal, you also have to keep in mind that the day still consists of only 24 hours. Therefore, you need to be selective with your choices, such that you allow yourself enough time to live a full life. Too often people dedicate most of their time to only one activity, which robs them of time for recuperation. In this respect, do your best to limit unnecessary activity in your line of work. A closer scrutiny of what really matters in what you do will help you determine those areas that can be trimmed out from your regular day: if you can save 5 minutes here and 5 minutes there, that will add up to a lot of time in the long run. The time you save can be used intelligently in other areas: family, personal development, taking responsibility for your own health, entertainment, and, also important, rejuvenation.

Pepper the 2nd

Smart time saving decisions can make the difference between success and failure. You may find it helpful to always search for constructive strategies that allow you to dedicate some time to additional hobbies other than your work. Changing the focus from your daily work to some less pressing activities is a great mental relaxation. After all, a rested mind performs better at crucially important tasks than a tired one. In fact, your brain cells structurally benefit by being engaged in treasured hobbies, as Dr. David Williams asserts in his May 2015 volume 18, No. 5, page 3, of Alternatives, For the Health Conscious Individual relative to learning something new regardless of how well is done.

That is where a wide range of possibilities come in. As you search for ways to refresh your energy, you should always look into those areas that interest you immediately secondary to your line of work. What is it you would like to do if it wasn't your present profession? Most likely those would be optimal candidates in your quest for hobbies. Many people prefer sports, music, long or short-term traveling, reading, writing, or arts and crafts, but if you like gardening, raising pets, fishing, or volunteering your time to worthwhile community causes, those could definitely be your choices.

After all, the idea is to have your heart in it such that at the end of the day you amass a significant amount of satisfaction that will constantly recharge you with positive energy. Most people are multitalented human beings. This implies that you should be able to derive pleasure and self-fulfillment from a variety of wisely selected activities, but in the meantime you should also be cautious in order to prevent burnouts. Yes, at times you might be tempted to do too much. And that is when your ability to set priorities comes very handy: select such that you have enough time for work, for family, for entertainment, for hobbies, and to get the needed rest. Be assured that your choices will direct your life according to their intended nature: nothing more, nothing less. Consequently, make sure your decisions are carefully thought out with positivity, such that your life flourishes with success and happiness.

30

My Math Calendar

The investigation of mathematical truths accustoms the mind to method and correctness in reasoning, and is an employment peculiarly worthy of rational beings.

George Washington

I have been teaching undergraduate mathematics in Austin, Texas, U.S.A. ever since 1982. Over the years, I accumulated my teaching experience at all three major levels of education: secondary (high school), two-year community college, and four-year university.

Based on my many years of teaching and realizing that there is a need for students to practice daily solving math problems, in 2013 I started work on a year-long calendar which is in fact a collection of mathematics problems at all undergraduate levels. Here is the introduction.

Math Calendar 2015

This calendar is meant to review mathematics concepts from basic to complex. Each page is dedicated to two days of the year and each day starts with a meaningful quotation followed by four problems. The first two are from developmental math, basic through intermediate algebra (up to high school algebra II), and the last two are from college credit mathematics, college algebra through calculus, progressing gradually from simple to complex throughout the year.

The main point of this daily setup is that the answers to the four problems are always found in the date (in this order): the month's number, the day's number, 20, and the number formed by the last two digits of the year (example: 2-14-20-15). Important note: the final answer should be the answer to the last question in every problem. Moreover, one can review (or learn) virtually all the undergraduate math concepts in 365 days over a set of 1,460 problems. Consequently, people interested in the developmental mathematics should focus on the first two daily problems, while those more advanced should focus on problems #3 and #4, using the first two as a warm-up.

The first suggestion I offer is obviously to solve the problems mentally (when possible) or by hand on a piece of paper, instead of checking to see if the answers given already work. Of course, at times one might need to review (or learn) some math concepts before attempting to solve a particular problem. However, as the calendar is also meant to improve number sense (a skill on the verge of extinction in modern education), hand-held calculators and computer software should be used minimally.

A second possible use of the calendar could be as an ordinary day planner. One could write notes and appointments in whatever empty space is available on each page.

And a third consideration should be given to the collection of problems itself. Since this set does review most of the undergraduate mathematics curriculum, it is perennial. One could find meaningful practice problems in this collection for years to come. Moreover, starting with 2017, I will be adjusting the problem set in new editions year after year such that it will keep functioning as a math calendar beyond 2015.

Important: most of the funds raised from the sales of this calendar will be donated to the Austin Community College (ACC) Scholarship Foundation meant to assist students in financial need and to reward ACC students participating in national college math competitions. In this respect, the calendar could be a constructive addition to help provide funding for programs at other educational institutions also.

Thank you for supporting this noble cause and enjoy your yearlong math experience.

Author: Irie Glajar
            Mathematics Professor
            Austin Community College
            irieg@austincc.edu
            http://mathcalendar.positive-imag-
ing.com.

31

Interview with Dr. Florin Bojor

The philosophy of the schoolroom in one generation will be the philosophy of government in the next.

Abraham Lincoln

It is fascinating to identify different academic practices, as we investigate this issue from institution to institution and from country to country. When we focus on mathematics, the differences are sometimes staggering. Since I completed my mathematics education in Romania in 1979, and I have been teaching college mathematics in Austin, Texas ever since 1984, I was obviously interested in updating my knowledge about the Romanian higher education in mathematics as it pertains to the new century. Part of the results of my search is summarized in this email interview on a few themes I found of interest.

Irie Glajar: Dr. Bojor, thank you very much for agreeing to this interview. Please tell us a little about your academic preparation, teaching position, and your place of employment.

Florin Bojor: I am Florin Bojor, mathematics professor at the National College Gheorghe Sincai, Baia Mare,

Romania, and it is my pleasure to participate in this interview. As to my academic preparation, I received my doctorate at the Technical University Cluj Napoca, University Center of North, Baia Mare, Department of Mathematics and Informatics.

IG: Please describe briefly the level of mathematical readiness of the high school graduates aspiring to Romanian universities.

FB: There is a difference between the requirements for the Baccalaureate Diploma and those for admittance to university as listed by the Ministry of Education; I will elaborate a little bit later.

IG: How was the admittance process to university structured before and after the 1989 Romanian Revolution?

FB: Before 1989 and a few years after, the admittance to the university was accomplished by a written exam, which was created by each individual institution. Once the private universities came on the scene, where the admittance is done by the student's grades from high school, a majority of state universities have adopted this admittance procedure. At this moment, there are only a few universities that require an admittance exam, namely to medicine and automation and informatics. The others conduct their admittance process based on the high school grades and the Baccalaureate result. In some cases there is a combination of the two, as students can opt for the exam. The exams themselves are based on the Baccalaureate curriculum but the actual problems are more difficult and in most cases are under the multiple-choice format, as opposed to the Baccalaureate exam where fully elaborated answers are expected.

IG: What are the specializations in higher education that your institution prepares students for in mathematics?

FB: Mathematics is a requirement at all specializations in mathematics, informatics, the technical universities, and economics.

IG: Please describe the structure of a course and the classroom activity in a higher education institution of mathematics in Romania.

FB: A university course consists of two 50-minute periods with a 10-minute break half way through. Each semester comprises 14 class meetings per subject of study, except mathematical analysis, which requires two meeting per week (28 class meetings per semester). Each course is accompanied by a seminary, a lab. Its focus is on applications based on the respective lectures, and where the homework is assigned. Attendance is not required but it is taken in consideration before the final grade is awarded.

IG: What is the examination and the grading system in such an institution?

FB: Grades are given from 10 (best) to 1 (lowest), with 5 being minimum passing. There are some subjects of study where there are partial exams throughout the semester, and others where there is only a final exam that consists of both theoretical and practical items. In mathematics there is less use of examination by essays.

IG: How is technology used in the process of teaching mathematics at a higher education institution in Romania?

FB: In the teaching activity computers are used rarely and only to run some files; pocket calculators are not used, and they are prohibited during exams. On the other hand, there are special courses on teaching the use of mathematical software such as Maple or Latex.

IG: Are there group-collaborative activities used in the classroom?

FB: In some subjects there are a number of proposed themes of study, students elect the theme they want to work on, they prepare it on their own time under a deadline, and then present it in front of the class and the professors, followed by open discussion.

IG: Finally, how do you see the Romanian higher education in mathematics from an international perspective?

FB: Internationally, the Romanian higher education in mathematics is not situated as high as the secondary education, which has very good international results. Statistically, the situation is not very good: there is no Romanian university ranked in the first 500 universities in the world. A very good reason for such low performance is the loss of many intelligent students who leave the country during or after high school (see the case of Omer Cerrahoglu).

I would like to thank Dr. Bojor for his time and for his thoughtful comments related to the higher education system in Romania, and to wish him all the best always.

32

Search for Beauty in the World

Man can only become what he is able to consciously imagine, or to "image forth."

Dane Rudhyar

As all of us humans are striving for wellbeing and happiness, it is only logical to seek those experiences that we believe more likely to generate such outcomes. In the meantime, the national media appears to focus mostly on the sad (negative) side of the news, and this seems to be the case around the world. For many years I watched international television news and read newspaper headlines, as my travels took me in many countries. I am saddened to say that yes, this is real: most media channels work for high ratings that can be achieved this way because a majority of people are attracted by the sensational side of life (usually negative events), being less interested in the positive, peaceful, and beautiful aspects of human existence.

Such thoughts found a welcoming home in my mind one night, as I was enjoying my regular walk around the neighborhood with Pepper the 3rd, my German-Shepherd. Under a fantastically clear full Moon and a sky decorated with stars that seemed close enough to pluck, in the comforting silence of the late night my being was immersed in a world of questions. As I was savoring the surreal beauty of that night's sky, the most insistent question in my mind was: why can't we focus more on the beauty of the world and the human being? For our own sake, why shouldn't we strive to build a life around that rather than on the poisonous message of sadness and despair fed through so many channels at all levels of human development? The answer came with no hesitation: exactly because many people have been conditioned this way by their choices. However, we have to realize that we are not condemned to live this reality for the rest of our lives; we can choose a better, more positive one, one that is filled with optimism and hope. By changing our attitudes and choices of action or inaction along with our day-by-day thoughts, we can reach this goal.

Indeed, there is so much beauty around us. All we need to do is find it, identify ourselves with it, and realize its immense potential to improve our lives. We will not be disappointed as we "slow down and smell the roses." Here are some examples of beauty in the society and the natural world.

1. **Human kindness**. Indeed, there is human kindness all around us and we need to set aside the time to identify it. One can witness the gratefulness of a homeless person at an intersection, as a driver hands out a dollar bill or an orange. That simple event can trigger a range of compassionate feelings in all witnesses, capable of causing deep personal transformations at the core level of human compassion. Along the same line, one can find many meaningful examples of human kindness, from the simple

helping an elderly person cross the street, to taking part in the remedy after major natural disasters. Life offers so many opportunities to manifest our humanness, and it seems shameful not to bring them forth as examples of truly positive human interaction they really are.

2. **Sunrises and sunsets.** It seems that the solar system conspires to offer us, the human beings, some of the most breath-taking views we can ever imagine. Every time I witness an exceptional sunrise or sunset, where the Sun is displaying its majesty through the beauty of the stratosphere of multicolored clouds, I say to myself: "Wow! What a picture! What a free and grandiose show we are handed!" and immediately I give thanks to that universal intelligence and order that sits calmly behind all things.

3. **Gardens.** From the famous Egyptian suspended gardens of thousands of years ago to the modern parks and gardens in most cities, one cannot but pay homage to the natural beauty of flower arrangements and design. Add to this the intrinsic beauty of the terrain decorated with beautiful rocks and sometimes secular trees, and you find some of the most impressive images one can search for in nature. Such surroundings are suitable to relaxation and meditation and can help reduce or eliminate stress and even the effects of illness.

The Balea Waterfall, Romania

4. **Mountains.** I am never so taken by scenery as I am by the beautiful and varied natural architecture of a mountain range. Anywhere in the world you might find yourself surrounded by mountains, the intimate details of the peaks, valleys, and vegetation are all different. That makes for a breath of fresh air figuratively and factually. From the many years when as a student I would spend my summer vacations in the mountains of Romania, to the more recent mountain adventure in Colorado, namely Pikes Peak, the rarified air and the capturing beauty of the scenery have had therapeutic effects on my entire being, physically and psychically.

5. **Music.** Regardless of what musical genre one might enjoy, it is a known fact that music can have a profound effect on people's wellbeing. Indeed, there is great beauty in music and it is fascinating to find that every person can identify that beauty in exactly the kinds of music they like. In fact, this is one of the greatest qualities of our world: diversity. So, every individual should be faithful to their own musical call and make the conscious effort to find and savor the beauty of each harmony that moves them.

6. **Sports.** Like music, sports affiliation constitutes another personal choice, and it plays more or less the same role. Whether one practices or just enjoys watching sports, is not important. What counts is the joy one gets in either situation. In this respect we can say for sure that people find great beauty in whatever sports they like. Thus, there are many optimal ways to search for relaxing and energizing entertainment.

7. **Art**. I don't think I need to remind anybody about the beauty of art. In fact, one can claim that this is a main motive for most art work: to display beauty. Museums are abundant all over the world in order to satisfy this imperious need of human beings for beauty, for uniqueness of ideas, and in the end, for education.

8. **Books**. As you read this book, you have just testified to the fact that books remain one of the most profound ways people seek beauty

in the world of ideas on a multitude of themes. Consequently, as we enter a bookstore, we are automatically driven to the sectors of books that interest us. Once again, it is personal, but nevertheless it is one of the most important sources of satisfaction people can find both in their search for entertainment and quest for education.

We can see, therefore, that the intrinsic human hunger for beauty needs to be intensified, away from the persistent and unfortunate appetite of modern media for the sensational, which often seems sad and downright frightening. The sources of beauty as we strive for happiness are abundant and the ones described above are just a few examples; each one of us can find their own. We can choose to reach out and embrace them, even though sometimes we may need to go out on a limb.

33

Choose Your Future: Be Happy Now!

Happiness is not a state to arrive at, but a manner of traveling.

Margaret Lee Runback

We were only three hours into the New Year 2014. I had just arrived home from what we in the Romanian traditional celebration of welcoming a new year called 'revelion.' It was very nice, at a restaurant in Austin, Texas, and one message that was unmistakably received by all was one of happiness. Resolutions ran wild. People had the wildest dreams for the New Year, some reasonable some not. But as I was observing the party, one revelation came clearly: we all seek happiness; not only on a New Year night but always!

It sounds very logical. Who wants to be unhappy? Even more, we can simply state that a meaning of life is to be happy; or as I often say, the meaning of life is JOY! In fact, it has been marked by ancient Egyptian tradition that, as a person was approaching the end of life, two questions were paramount regarding chances for the soul to reach heaven: did they have joy in life, and did their lives bring joy to others? What a great way to summarize an earthly existence!

Along these lines I propose the obvious, namely we all pursue a happy life. I know: we all do. However, many of us choose to schedule this for tomorrow. Considerably too often I have heard people say "I will do so much better when ..." or "I will be so happy when ..." forgetting that 'when' could actually be NOW! 'When' will never come unless we pass through NOW. 'When' is so elusive that we cannot count on it NOW; nobody can. All we have is in fact NOW. The past has passed and no future is guaranteed. Moreover, NOW starts the rest of our lives. All that will come will be based on NOW in a very well defined cause-and-effect series of interconnected live events that will decide the rest of our existence. So, a conclusion makes itself obvious: why not start the 'being happy project' NOW?

Really! Why not living every minute of our lives as the only one we have? In fact it is true: neither the past nor the future are consciously lived in the present moment. Based on this realization, make a choice to be happy NOW. And no, it is not as abstract as it seems. All of us, with the power of choosing what to think at our discretion, can make this self-talk decision:

I WILL NOT LET NEGATIVITY INTERFERE WITH MY HAPPINESS! Or,

REGARDLESS OF CIRCUMSTANCES, I CHOOSE HAPPINESS AND WELLBEING!

In his book *Most of All They Taught Me Happiness*, Dr. Robert Muller, who has made extensive and meaningful contributions to the successful worldwide activities of the United Nations, enlists an abundance of lessons he received throughout his life on how to be happy. Subtitles such as "Happy Even in Prison," "Of Laughter," "Of Daily Blessings," "Of Simplicity," and

"A Moral and Spiritual Dimension," stand out in a cluster of inspirational essays that illustrate themes like lessons learned from the war (the Second WW), adulthood, nature, the elders, world trade, and of course the United Nations. The underlined message is beautifully crafted from his vast range of experiences around the world and it is as simple as it is convincing. In spite of the circumstances in which we find ourselves, we always have the choice of giving in to despair and agony, or to embrace happiness, in the understanding that everything that comes our way is actually an opportunity.

Indeed, it is all up to us, and examples abound. The fact is that we live within a universe of cause and effect, so, what we do today unmistakably affects what we will experience in the future. It might not be tomorrow or even this year, but there is no way around it. And in case of doubt, we can prove it to ourselves simply by looking into our own past: aren't we today the result of our previous choices? We are; good, bad, or neutral, but we are. This realization can pave the road to what we really long for in the future. Do we choose happiness, health, relaxation, and fulfilled dreams, or do we just let ourselves be at the mercy of the circumstances coming our way? One age-old saying comes to mind: as you think so shall you be. How true! Can it be any other way, since everything we experience is of our own making? To understand this, just try to remember every single choice you have made so far in your life: it is impossible. Consequently, while under this understanding we cannot legitimately claim victimhood, the choice is clear: we should assume responsibility for everything that touches our lives. We should learn our lessons, and choose today only that which makes us happy. Of course, such choices should not be made at the expense of others, as we should observe the law of cause and effect at work for our own sake.

Mosu

Another great example of a dedicated but not pretentious proponent of happiness is that of my grandfather on my father's side. Mosu (the 'Old One'), as we affectionately called him, was born in 1902 in Romania, grew up in a peasant family, completed only two years of formal elementary education, and in the 1930s had his passport ready to come to the United States of America to work. His aim was to return home with enough money to buy land and build a farm to support his family. However, the start of unrest in Europe and eventually the Second WW prevented him from leaving, so he had to manage with what he had. And it was all good up to 1962 when the totalitarian communist regime of Romania nationalized by force virtually every acre of cultivatable land in the country. Mosu was no exception: he lost everything (for details please see *Escape to Freedom,* my autobiography). But even so, he never lost his great joy of singing Romanian folklore pertaining to his region, Southern Transylvania. Ever since I can remember, his singing voice was the unmistakable sign of happiness usually while working. How else should one describe it if not as love for life, and this in spite of him loosing basically all he owned, as the communists nationalized everything? Yes, he suffered deeply at the family loss, but he got right back on his feet and made the best of it. Neighbors, relatives, and friends would savor the working atmosphere he would create especially with his singing. That had the unseen power to soften somewhat the general pain that had marked everyone's life at the hands of the Romanian dictatorial regime. Mosu was the embodiment of optimism as he refused to offer himself as prey to sadness and despair. Within a regimen of hard work in the fields, this time for the government, he had found a sensitive avenue, through his music, to function and be happy. And those were not sad songs. No. Especially for his co-workers audience (although I heard him singing happy songs even working alone), he would select cheerful repertoire instinctively knowing how much people needed the uplifting. In retrospect, I can definitely say that Mosu had made the choice for happiness regardless of the circumstances. He lived that way until his last week, the only week in his life he was confined to a bed, before he died in December 1974. In fact, and in spite of his rejection of the communist takeover, some of his last words on his death-bed were: "I will be missing this world!"

With examples such as the ones I included here, I think it is simply a matter of our choices as we are crafting our future. For a happy future we should be happy now. 'Now' is the only time we really have and it is up to us how we use it. There is plenty of inspiration all around us. It comes in diverse forms, such as from nature, books, videos, music, movies, plays, and many other sources. We can find that inspiration and we should treasure every chance we have to share it with others, as we attempt to deepen our own states of happiness: I am doing this right now with this book! After all, as I said before, joy can easily describe in a concise but beautiful way the meaning of human life. Therefore, we should never abandon our efforts to nurture happiness today in order to enjoy it tomorrow.

34

Epilogue

Dream lofty dreams, and as you dream, so shall you become.
Your vision is the promise of what you shall at last unveil.

John Ruskin

Or instead of Epilogue, I would propose "Setting up a personal HPH project." What do I mean by this? In light of most of the essays presented here and in my book *Teach For Life*, I would like to suggest a permanent strategy summarized into three components: Health, Prosperity, and Happiness, hence HPH.

I believe health is the precursor of wellbeing. Consequently, we should design for ourselves a life regimen that supports this ideal: be healthy. By this I mean to focus on physical health, emotional health, and psychological health. To accomplish it we should watch carefully our diet and simultaneously do the best we can to follow a regular program of some form of physical exercise. From brisk walking, jogging and running, to team sports, weight lifting, yard work, and yoga, as well as other physical activities we enjoy, could be made part of our lives. At the same time, we should closely monitor our emotions; kept in balance, emotions can help us with respect to whatever endeavors we engage ourselves in. Extreme emotions, either of sadness or excitement can, more often than not, undermine our wellbeing. Considering psychological health, we should constantly monitor our thoughts in order to send ourselves, and allow us to receive, only those messages that ensure peace of mind and self-confidence. Conscious efforts on these three fronts can assist us on the road to proper overall health.

Prosperity can be easily misunderstood when one thinks only of riches. What I mean by prosperity is that level of personal financial status that makes us content in life. Some desire more, some less. It is all in order as long as we are satisfied. However, I believe that to accomplish certain goals we do need a corresponding financial platform; a case can be made for philanthropy, for example, since we cannot give that what we don't possess. In this respect, as most people understand, a proven way to increase our chances for an adequate financial status is definitely education. Therefore, we should use whatever educational avenues possible and make necessary sacrifices in order to reach the particular academic or trade level of readiness required in the field of our choice. In other words, find what we really like to do, acquire the proper education and training, and dedicate ourselves to the success of our mission. Prosperity will follow as long as our efforts are directed to serving the society that allows us the freedom to exercise our creativity.

And then, be happy all along. Indeed, happiness is not the destination, but it is a state of being. Our HPH project should always be centered on happiness, and in the process we can actually make happiness (or joy) the meaning of our lives. As each of us is a unique human being, of course the manifestation of happiness varies from person to person. Some seem to be happy by nature, while most of us need to consciously work on it. Some are happy with little, while some need more. That is definitely fine. As long as we seek happiness without hurting anyone or the environment in the process, we should be free on our path. After all, we are both responsible for, and in charge of how we choose to react with respect to our circumstances. Therefore, we should exercise our control and accept the consequences. That is possibly the best way to help ourselves create the life we desire, and along the way help others do the same in their own lives.

I wish you well!

About the Author

Irie Glajar was born in Communist Romania in 1955, has graduated from the University of Cluj, Romania with a Master's degree in Mathematics and Computer Science in 1979, and defected from the dictatorial regime in 1981. After several months in an Italian political refugee camp he immigrated into the United States of America and since September 1982 has been teaching undergraduate mathematics at both high school and college levels in Austin, Texas. In 2010 Mr. Glajar earned an additional Master's degree in Mathematics Education from The University of North, Baia Mare, Romania.

Over the years, he has participated and presented at many professional conferences in the U.S., Canada, and Romania, and published several educational articles both in the U.S. and Romania. After the 2007 publication of his first book *"WE ARE ALL ONE, The End of All Worries: Scientific and Spiritual Testimonies to the Unity of All Things,"* the author published *"TEACH FOR LIFE, Essays on Modern Education For Teachers, Students, and Parents."* He continued with *"ESCAPE TO FREEDOM, Chronicles of a Life on Two Continents, My Escape from Communist Romania, An Autobiography,"* followed by the publication of his *"2015 INSPIRATIONAL MATHEMATICS CALENDAR AND DAY PLANNER"* which is a collection of 1460 undergraduate math problems from basic to complex, spread as four problems per day with their answers in the re-spective date. And, under the title *"EDUCATION IN A CHANGING WORLD,"* Irie's present collection of 34 essays proposes a variety of ideas on teaching and learning for a better life.

Besides treasuring his family life and his teaching career at Austin Community College, Austin, Texas, Irie Glajar finds much satisfaction in hobbies such as music, gardening, pets, and sports. Along with sci-ences and philosophy, he is also deeply interested in metaphysics, religion, spirituality, and international travel, which provide constant inspiration for his teaching of mathematics and his vision of modern ed-ucation at large.

Irie Glajar can be contacted via email at: ir_gl@yahoo.com.

Bibliography

Augros, Robert M. and Stanciu, George N.

 The New Story of Science. Bantam Books, 1984.

Capra, Fritjof.

 The Tao of Physics. Shambhala, 1991.

Chopra, Deepak.

 Quantum Healing. Harmony Books.

Cook, John.

 The Book of Positive Quotations. Gramercy Books, 1993.

Dossey, Larry.

 Science, Spirit, & Soul. Sounds True, Audio tape.

Dyer, Wayne W.

 What do You Really Want for Your Children. Avon Books.

 Applying the Wisdom of the Ages. Nightingale Conant, Audio tapes.

Dyer, Wayne W. & Chopra, Deepak.

 Creating Your World the Way You Really Want It to Be. Hay House, Inc.

Einstein, Albert.

 Science and Religion. Crown Publishers.

 Ideas and Opinions. Wings Books, 1954.

Fox, Matthew and Sheldrake, Rupert.

The Sacred Universe. Sounds True, Audio tapes, 1993.

Fromm, Erich.

The Art of Loving. Harper & Brothers Publishers, 1956.

Lederman, Leon.

The God Particle. Houghton Mifflin Company, 1993

MacLaine, Shirley.

Out on a Limb. Bantam Books.

Muller, Robert.

Most of All They Taught Me Happiness. AMARE MEDIA LLC, 2005.

Ram Dass.

Be Here Now. Crown Publishing.

Rochlin, Gene I.

Trapped in the Net. Princeton University Press, 1997.

Rucker, Rudy.

Infinity and the Mind. Bantam Books, Inc., 1983.

Sheldrake, Rupert.

The Rebirth of Nature. Bantam Books, Inc., 1991.

Shenk, David.

Data Smog. HarperCollins Publishers, 1997.

Sommer, Bobbe.

Psycho-Cybernetics, 2000. Prentice Hall, 1993.

Stoll, Clifford.

High Tech Heretic. Anchor Books, 2000.

Talbot, Michael.

The Holographic Universe. HarperCollins Publishers.

Beyond the Quantum. Bantam Books.

Zukarov, Gary.

The Dancing Wu Li Masters. Bantam Books, 1979.

Walsch, Neale Donald.

Conversations with God – an uncommon dialogue – Books 1, 2, 3. Hampton Roads Publishing Company. Inc., 1996, 1997, 1998.

Wilber, Ken.

Quantum Questions. Shambhala, 1985.

Wilson, Edward O.

The Meaning of Human Existence. Liveright Publishing Corporation, 2015.